30 Satires

# 30 Satires

◆

LEWIS LAPHAM

**THE NEW PRESS**

NEW YORK
LONDON

Requests for permission to reproduce selections from this book should be mailed to:
Permissions Department, The New Press, 38 Greene Street, New York, NY 10013

Published in the United States by The New Press, New York, 2005
Distributed by W. W. Norton & Company, Inc., New York

LIBRARY OF CONGRESS CATALOGING-IN-PUBLICATION DATA

Lapham, Lewis H.
    30 satires / Lewis Lapham.
       p.   cm.
    ISBN 1-56584-846-2 (hc.) ISBN 1-56584-986-8 (pbk.)
    I. Title: Thirty satires. II. Title.

PS3612.A64A614 2003
814'.54—dc21

2003050951

The New Press was established in 1990 as a not-for-profit alternative to the large,
commercial publishing houses currently dominating the book publishing industry.
The New Press operates in the public interest rather than for private gain, and is
committed to publishing, in innovative ways, works of educational, cultural, and
community value that are often deemed insufficiently profitable.

*Composition by Westchester Book Composition*

Printed in the United States of America

2   4   6   8   10   9   7   5   3   1

# Contents

# Author's Note

"Well, humor is the great thing, the saving thing, after all."
MARK TWAIN

Whether humor saves the reader or the country, I have no way of knowing and cannot say, but for the writer of the pages in this book, it's the door left open in the wall of cant and the way out of the fog of lies. Laughter cannot help but breathe the air of freedom, by its nature deaf to the voices of indoctrination or command, and I trust the joke to strike more nearly at the truth than the sermon, the sales pitch or the State of the Union address. Satire makes alliance with the spirit of dissent and arms the writer with the hope of a possible escape from his own stupidity and fear. Any reader who finds in these inventions something of the same happy prospect will have put them to their intended use.

# Christmas Carol

You can tell the ideals of a nation by its advertisements.
—NORMAN DOUGLAS

Wandering among the remote shelves of a Fifth Avenue bookstore in late October, I came across a small stack of books on the floor near a freight elevator, ten or twelve copies of a cheaply printed paperback bound up with string and marked with a slip of paper identifying them as goods in transit. Assuming that they were what was left of the summer's best-selling news about the O. J. Simpson trial, and curious to see which authors and what theories of criminal justice were being returned to pulp, I lifted the corner of the invoice and was surprised to find Charles Dickens's *A Christmas Carol* in a red cover with the familiar illustration of Mr. Fezziwig's ball. I had mistaken the direction of the shipment. Books that I had thought were going out were coming in, but the sales clerks apparently hadn't decided where to place what the publisher's tag line described as "the most beloved Christmas tale of them all."

As I continued to browse among the season's newest political tracts, many of them about bringing discipline to the nation's economy and strengthening its penal codes, it occurred to me that maybe the clerks were embarrassed by the mawkish sentimentality of the beloved tale. Maybe they were reluctant to display it in the front of a store that undoubtedly numbered among its patrons quite a few corporate managers apt to possess precisely those qualities that Dickens so deplored in Ebenezer Scrooge—"Hard and sharp as flint, from which no steel had ever struck out generous fire, secret, and self-contained, and solitary as an oyster." It won't do these days to make a mockery of wealth or portray a rich businessman as anything other than a hero of the people. Money is the proof of grace, and a miser, as every schoolchild knows, is a great and good conservative. The plotline of A *Christmas Carol* didn't fit the bracing spirit of the times, and neither did its irresponsible moral lesson. Here was old Scrooge, an exemplary Republican, troubled in his sleep by ghostly dreams of human kindness, changed into a gibbering liberal at the sight of a crippled child. Hardly an inspiring tale of triumphant profit-taking and certainly not one that anybody would want to place next to a handsome photograph of Newt Gingrich or Peter Lynch.

Sensitive to the predicament of the sales staff, I wondered whether it might be possible to rewrite A *Christmas Carol* in a way that more nearly matched the forthright, manly teaching of the Contract with America. Not an easy revision, of course, and one that would require some fairly heavy-handed deconstruction of the text, but after a few moments' thought, and taking heart from the brisk sales at the cash register of *Beyond Prozac* and *Your*

*Sacred Self*, I understood that the tale was probably best retold as a sequel. As follows:

## STAVE I

Our story begins with the appalling sight of Ebenezer T. Scrooge V, a benign and mild-mannered man in his late fifties, generous to a fault, who for many years has been squandering his great-great-grandfather's noble fortune on misguided schemes to rescue the unrepentant poor. The imbecile philanthropist sits reading a romantic novel by Leo Tolstoy in a small but cheerful library surrounded by the worthless tokens of an idealist's misspent life— photographs signed by Mahatma Gandhi, Gary Hart, and Hillary Clinton, civic awards mounted in second-rate silver, a pet owl, forgotten reports from forgotten presidential commissions appointed to study racial injustice and environmental disgrace, Mark Twain's walking stick, books published by Marxist university professors, framed letters of appreciation from the students of an elementary school in Ciudad Juárez, a bowl of Hudson River mud.

It is the hour after sunset on Christmas Eve, and the rest of the house is full of music and light. The children and grandchildren of Ebenezer Scrooge V, all of them too careless with money (too careless by far) and too easily moved to laughter (to the point of impertinence), have invited so many guests to dinner that they can't remember how many places to set at the table. They make a joyful noise of their preparations, the clattering of plates and the popping of champagne corks joined with the sound of a piano and three voices singing "God Rest Ye Merry Gentlemen."

The ghost of Jacob Marley drifts through the library door looking as dismal as it looked in London in 1843, "like a bad lobster
in a dark cellar," but instead of being weighted down with heavy
locks and chains, the apparition takes the form of a scolding family
lawyer come to correct the spendthrift heir with the switch of
sound advice. Scrooge suggests a glass of wine, "a little something
to restore the color to your cheeks," but Marley waves the offer
impatiently aside and reminds the descendant of his former partner that the money is all but gone, the trust funds nearly exhausted, and the warehouses on the verge of bankruptcy. Before
floating out the window, the ghost tells Scrooge to expect three
unearthly visitors, three spirits who, if he heeds them well, will
recall him to the bosom of Mammon.

## STAVE II

The Ghost of Christmas Past bears a remarkable resemblance
to John D. Rockefeller, the founder of the fortune of that name
and known during his long and grasping life as the incarnation
of stinginess. Somber as a pallbearer, looking more like a starved
New England clergyman than a well-fed financier, the ghost bids
Scrooge rise from his chair and walk with him in the night sky
on a grand tour of America as it existed a hundred years ago, the
old, economically competitive America, innocent of labor unions
and free of feminists. The spirit shows Scrooge a series of canonical
scenes: gangs of Chinese laborers laying railroad track across the
Nevada desert, handsome policemen mounted on thoroughbred
horses suppressing Irish mobs, criminals on treadmills, unheated
shoe factories in the dead of winter, the children bent to their

tasks in orderly and uncomplaining rows, patriotic newspapermen wearing checked suits and bowler hats, bowing like Kewpie dolls to the magnates of the Gilded Age, grim country parsons singing psalms, picturesque beggars in sprightly rags, indigent pensioners dying as unobtrusively as flies, too proud of their American heritage (independent and self-reliant) to bother anybody with a plea for help or a cry of pain.

Presented as an album of prints by Currier & Ives, the little scenes blink on and off at regular intervals through the scudding cloud, and to each of them the Ghost of Christmas Past affixes, like a Christmas ribbon or a sprig of holly, the ornament of an edifying thought:

"Beware, Ebenezer Scrooge, the ageless ingratitude of the poor."

"Never show sympathy to people from whom you can expect nothing in return."

"Charity destroys initiative and rots the will to industry and enterprise."

Scrooge stands abashed before the solemn images of frugality and thrift. For the first time in his wastrel's life, he begins to apprehend the majesty of a cold and savage heart, and when the spirit returns him to the comfort of his library he glances at the fire burning on the hearth and thinks that it would cast a purer light with one log instead of four.

## STAVE III

No sooner has the clock struck the hour of ten than the Ghost of Christmas Present rises up through the floor like the genie from Aladdin's Lamp—a figure not dissimilar to that of Rush Limbaugh or Roseanne—grinning, corpulent, and huge, the soul of perfect selfishness. Dressed in a loose gown of flowered silk and wearing on its gigantic head a crown of cloves and pineapples, the apparition claps Scrooge boisterously on the back and announces, amid gusts of booming laughter, that it has come to teach the lessons of gratified desire. Only fools and saints and New Deal Democrats subordinate their own comforts to those of others or put off until tomorrow pleasures that can be seized today. So saying, and as if to prove its point, the great spirit seizes Scrooge by the wrist, drags him upward through the roof, and spreads before him a second panoramic view of America the Beautiful. Once again the purpose is didactic, but instead of dwelling on the triumphs of the past, the genie of the shopper's lamp displays the glories of the miraculous present. The settings are all suburban— office parks and shopping malls, resort communities protected by high walls and iron gates, ski lodges, university quadrangles, boat marinas. No black or brown people appear anywhere in sight— no red or yellow people, nobody wearing rings in his ear or her nose, no loud musical instruments, no government bureaucrats, no street vendors selling filthy foreign foods. All the factories have been turned into overpriced restaurants, all the assembly lines neatly trimmed and downsized (like the hedges at the entrance of a good hotel), all the IRS agents turned into tennis instructors or personal trainers.

Enfolding Scrooge within the giant arc of its ham-like arm, and with a chuckle as merry as the holiday catalogue from Bloomingdale's, the Ghost of Christmas Present invites him to gaze upon the prizes that money buys for people mature enough to know that in the end and when all is said and done (no matter what happens to anybody in Bosnia or Queens), they have only themselves to please. From the depths of the now starry night a magnificent procession of shining luxuries floats before Scrooge's eyes, and as the objects pass splendidly by, the great spirit names them as the orphaned pleasures that Scrooge has foolishly forsworn.

The last yacht and the last cashmere cap drift slowly away to the south, and Scrooge once again discovers himself in his library listlessly turning the pages of a book that suddenly seems as dingy and old as Leo Tolstoy's beard. It occurs to him that maybe he has lived too long in the company of the dispossessed. As a child he had known about the marble fountains and the heavy motor cars, and he had seen magazine advertisements for the racehorses and Italian suits, but the second unearthly visitor had surprised him with some of the newer and more complicated toys—menageries of tame politicians in silver cages, miniature billionaires no bigger than fawns, newspaper editors cleverly contrived to sing like the golden, mechanical birds once made for the amusement of Oriental princes.

## STAVE IV

In the hour before midnight the Spirit of Christmas Yet to Come, an ominous and silent figure in a black shroud, summons Scrooge with the gesture of one outstretched hand—a hand as pale as death—to the French doors leading out into the rose garden. Scrooge has by now become wary of strange sights. Guessing at the nature of the dreadful entertainment likely to appear among the rosebushes, he rises unwillingly from his chair, afraid to look

upon the face of doom. In a small and creeping voice he asks for
program notes: "You are about to show me shadows of things that
have not happened but will happen in the time before us? Is that
so, Spirit?"

The phantom neither speaks nor moves. The outstretched hand
draws back the curtain of the night, and the garden blooms with
scenes of pandemonium that look like they might have been
jointly painted by Jan Brueghel and Hieronymus Bosch: the entire
population of Oklahoma stoned on drugs and heavy metal rock
bands loose in the Iowa corn, undocumented aliens disembarking
from ships (like the animals descending from Noah's ark) in every
port on the once well-defended American coast, unemployed corporate executives (white and middle-aged) selling apples on the
steps of the Pentagon, lewd women (as young and licentious as
Calvin Klein's child models, as old and insatiable as the Wife of
Bath) selling sexual favors in Harvard Yard, gay and lesbian pa-
rades in Salt Lake City, debates in Congress conducted in gangsta
rap, fifth-grade classrooms studying the history of pornographic
film (a twenty-seven-part series produced by the Public Broadcasting System and narrated by Bill Moyers), shiftless fathers
throwing away their children like empty beer cans, unwed moth-
ers nursing unbaptised infants on the floor of the New York Stock
Exchange, altar boys spinning roulette wheels and nobody reading
William Bennett's *Book of Virtues,* young black men in velvet top
hats standing around on street corners frightening the police.

Scrooge cannot bear to look upon the dreadful scene for more
than twenty minutes. He falls trembling to his knees, clutching
at the phantom's robe. "Hear me, good Spirit. Why show me this

if I am past all hope? I am not the man I was. I will not be the man I must have been but for this gift of Phil Gramm's grace."

The phantom departs as silently as it came, and the exhausted Scrooge falls into a fitful sleep, dreaming of reform schools.

## STAVE V

Faithful to the miracle of redemption, Scrooge awakens on Christmas morning restored to the winter glory of his ancestors— his cheeks noticeably shriveled, his blood four degrees colder in his stiffened veins, a suddenly squeezing, wrenching, envious man whose movements have become as quick and nervous as a lizard's tongue. At last Scrooge has come to know the meaning of a dollar and the beauty of the bottom line. In a hurry to be up and dressed, his hands busy with his shirt and tie while at the same time talking on a cellular phone, he cancels the clown ordered for a children's cancer ward, instructs his brokers to buy shares in companies that own and manage prisons, orders the closing of seven factories, chases out of the house the company of useless guests, berates the cook (for putting too much stuffing in the Christmas turkey), disinherits his grandchildren, and sells the owl. Later in the morning, on the way to his office in New York City, Scrooge walks briskly north on Fifth Avenue, shaking his shrunken fists at the Christmas wreaths but coveting, like any other loyal American, all the precious merchandise in all the better stores. Asked for money at the corner of Fifty-seventh Street by a crippled child as surely doomed as Tiny Tim Cratchit, Scrooge rebukes the waif for its insolence and kicks away its crutch.

*December 1995*

# The Last Hohenzollern

If we would please in society, we must be prepared to be
taught many things we know already by people
who do not know them.
—CHAMFORT

For another season at least, possibly through the whole of
the summer and maybe into the fall, it apparently will
remain obligatory at the better parties in Washington and
New York to say something intelligible about the hydrogen
bomb. As a topic of required conversation the bomb has had an
eccentric history, and it is not always easy to know how to conduct
oneself in its sullen presence.

During the late 1950s the bomb was very much in vogue and
often in the news. Everybody who was anybody wanted to be seen
thinking or talking about it. But then, soon after Richard Nixon
was elected president, and for reasons never satisfactorily explained, the bomb dropped from sight, and nobody thought to
ask where it went. Presumably it had taken an extended leave of
absence. Maybe it had been granted tenure at one of those strategic

institutes in California; possibly it had gone off with the last hippies on the gypsy wagons of the counterculture. For ten years everybody who was anybody forgot what it looked like and why it was so important.

With the advent of the Reagan Administration the topic staged a triumphant return. As ugly and unthinkable as always, but dressed in a wardrobe of modish abstraction, it was at first seen mostly in the company of the left. The apostles of peace and disarmament, deeply embarrassed by the Republican Risorgimento, once again had a heroic friend that could rescue them from obscurity and anomie. Jonathan Schell wrote a hymn to the bomb's omnipotence entitled *The Fate of the Earth*, and Carl Sagan assembled a triptych, not unlike those painted by Hieronymus Bosch, entitled "Nuclear Winter." The journals of advanced literary opinion presented shows of pious alarm. The popular media took the topic around to folk festivals and rallies in Central Park, introducing it to Baryshnikov, Barbara Walters, and Sam Shepard. Among its admirers on the left, the bomb invariably attains the status of celebrity, a romantic persona comparable to that of a French film director who requires a limousine and flowers in his suite at the St. Regis.

The fierce professors on the militant right prefer to think of the bomb as German royalty, perhaps the last of the Hohenzollerns, but in any event an extremely austere personage wearing a high starched collar and not amused by small talk. By the autumn of 1983 they had managed to shift the conversation from disarmament to the Strategic Defense Initiative (a.k.a. "Star Wars"), substituting magical promises of an invincible shield for gloomy presentiments of the apocalypse. At an arms control conference some months ago in Washington a woman made the mistake of asking a question about certain technical aspects of nuclear strategy. Her impertinence annoyed Donald Regan, the president's chief of staff. Rising to the defense of the bomb's dignity, Regan said, testily: "Women don't know anything about throw weights."

The subtleties of nuclear etiquette—obviously more complicated than they might seem—cannot be acquired as readily as a new dress or a New York City politician. As has been said, the proper attitude toward the topic varies with the company it keeps. Because it is sometimes difficult to think of a suitable phrase or inflection of the voice, and because the topic might remain current until Christmas, I have made a few notes about the protocols likely to be deemed both safe and socially correct:

1. On being seated next to the topic at dinner, refrain from making jokes. Whether approached from the left or the right, the nuclear holocaust is a very serious and very ponderous guest. It doesn't speak English. The tone of address should be respectful, as if you were conversing with Alexander Haig or a large sum of money. Laughter and rude remarks will mark you as a person of low birth.

2. The topic is always in impeccable taste. Mention your acquaintance with it at every possible opportunity, and nobody can find fault with the interior decoration of your soul. You have chosen the best. What can be more important than the end of the world?

3. Sign all petitions circulated by the appropriate authorities. If you believe in a nuclear freeze, you can join
   committees of concerned authors, artists, and Nobel
   laureates. Your name might appear in a newspaper advertisement with the names of Barbra Streisand and
   Kurt Vonnegut. The billing can't do you any harm with
   the Internal Revenue Service, and it might get you invited to a party in East Hampton. If the committee asks
   for money, calculate the sum of your contribution by
   counting the number of celebrities listed on the letterhead and multiplying the result by $20.

   If you believe in the miracle of "Star Wars," sign
   any piece of paper submitted by a quorum of retired
   Air Force generals. Your name will appear on a White
   House mailing list, and you might be invited to sub-
   scribe to *Commentary* or *National Review*.

4. Because of its ecumenical nature, the topic of the bomb
   absorbs and nullifies all the moral passion previously
   invested in the issues of civil rights, women's rights,
   Vietnam, Watergate, the deficit, affirmative action, government regulation, pornography, and the environment.

5. A noble preoccupation with the nuclear holocaust ex-
   cuses your ignorance of lesser evils and explains your
   indifference to death caused by conventional weapons.
   The Soviet Union routinely sponsors the murder of un-
   ruly citizens, and the Israeli government, while "mopping up" Palestinian strongholds in Tunisia or Lebanon,

sometimes has occasion to kill an impressive number of civilians. The victims die without benefit of radiation and thus do not merit much notice in the press.

6. If the conversation takes a nasty turn in the direction of the host's thievery in the stock market, you can interrupt and say, "Yes, of course, but when one thinks of it in terms of 10 million deaths . . ." The same strategy can be employed to divert the small talk away from the sexual chicanery taking place among the guests at the other end of the table.

7. The topic allows you to think only about important people—generals, best-selling prophets, national security advisers, film stars, television broadcasters, heads of state. You needn't give much thought to the teeming mob of the world's poor. They, too, will be consumed in the nuclear fire, but they can't do anything about it, and their departure will be met with as little interest as their arrival.

8. The topic is restful. It stimulates anxiety about a catastrophe that has yet to happen. This is the most comfortable form of despair, far more convenient than trying to deal with a catastrophe already in progress (e.g., the public schools).

9. If somebody asks you to recommend a course of action, you need not worry about your lack of suggestion. None of the best people know what to do. It is no disgrace

to confess your helplessness, but you must do so with an air of profound regret, which, if managed correctly, signifies your appreciation of modernism.

10. On weekends in the country the topic likes to read the Sunday papers and go for long walks. It doesn't play tennis.

*May 1986*

# *Philosopher Kings*

Professor Stephen Wilkes
Department of Literature
University of California, Santa Cruz
1156 High Street
Santa Cruz, CA 95064-1077

Dear Professor Wilkes,

I appreciate your kind word about *Harper's Magazine*, and I take it as a compliment that you should think to send me a copy of your remarks to the Santa Barbara symposium on the topic "The American Public Intellectual: An Endangered Species." I don't doubt that your presentation was well-received, and I can see why you would think it "of particular interest to an editor mindful of the veil of darkness descending on the nation's political discourse." I admire your erudition and share your wish that both Walter Lippmann and Bernard de Voto were writing a Sunday column for the *New York Times*, but I think that you carry the symposium's subtitle too far into the forests of metaphor. We are not talking about "the loss of a natural resource as precious as the High Plains aquifer," much less the "fast-disappearing song of the Kirtland's warbler." We're talking about academic careerists auditioning for the voices of Moses or Cardinal de Richelieu.

Forgive the sarcasm. Probably I've met too many would-be public intellectuals, and I tend to think of them as people from whom one does well to hide. During the early years of the first Clinton Administration I attended a number of conferences similar to the one at which you gave your remarks; Clinton was fond of what were known at the time as "multiparticipant discussion threads," and the organizers of weekend retreats at Colonial Williamsburg and Hilton Head liked to dress up the program with topics bearing on the quality control of American public opinion—depth of meaning and degrees of importance, conditions of manufacture and terms of sale, problems presented by the repackaging of high-end political theory for down-market distribution. Although I took careful notes and didn't neglect the portfolio of helpful study materials (readings from the works of Cicero, John Locke, George Orwell, et al.), I never learned to draw the fine distinctions between the public and the private interest—what was good for America as opposed to what was good for the panelist promoting his or her new book, on sale in the hotel lobby and coming soon to a neighborhood PBS station. I undoubtedly missed many subtle references and far-reaching ramifications, but the conference summary always seemed to me pretty straightforward:

A. The American citizenry has been reduced to a herd of lascivious sheep.

B. The herd requires guidance and direction.

C. Who better to provide guidance and direction than those of us here in the Sea Island Room?

D. Happily for the safety of the Republic, we're not the kind of people who covet riches or seek the glow of celebrity. We don't mind standing slightly behind the podium, imparting knowledge, pointing out the way to the just society, the best restaurants, the City on the Hill.

E. If America doesn't come quickly to its senses, doesn't begin to read our books, how can we defend its treasured freedoms and priceless cultural heritage against the devastation of CNN and MTV?

I stopped going to the conferences shortly after Clinton was elected to a second term, but I continue to receive transcripts of some of the proceedings, and judging by your own text as well as what I read in the journals of upscale political opinion, the tone and substance of the hypothesis hasn't changed much over the last ten years. The country still flounders in the morass of dumbed-down journalism and bad television (your own point about the summer ratings for *Fear Factor*), and where is Ralph Waldo Emerson?

Maybe you could answer the question, Professor, but why the hope of rescue from the universities? From the universities and literary persons familiar with the writings of Theodor Adorno and Louis-Ferdinand Céline? Why the presumption that when searching for the lost public intellectual, we should be poking around

Harvard Square or looking under the desks at *The New York Review of Books?*

If I read correctly your pages eight through twelve, you have reasons of your own to doubt the claims of the academy to the throne of wisdom. You compare the faculty deans of your acquaintance to "dead moons circling a burnt-out sun"; you speak of "envious and embittered pedants" so preoccupied with departmental politics that they cannot see beyond "the narrow horizon of their futile specialties." Not the best of circumstances for the restoration of the ancient Greek agora, but your description agrees with what little I know of universities from my own brief observations as a guest lecturer and from many years of wandering in the desert of tenured prose. When I read the books by academic authors mourning the emptiness of the public square, I seldom come away convinced that the country stands in dire peril; I'm left instead with the impression that the self-appointed guardians of the nation's conscience wish to be consulted on matters that almost none of them understand.

The expectation of a civic reawakening in the literary professions seems to me even more recklessly misplaced. The joke would come clearer to you, Professor, if you could spend some time in close confinement with the New York media crowd. Everybody has a brilliant opinion; everybody can go the distance of three sentences on any topic that comes into the room with the bearded movie critic or the shredded pork. Three sentences on the whereabouts of Chandra Levy, on the war in Israel, free-range lettuce, cyberspace, the San Andreas Fault, the sadness of autumn in the Balkans. But that's it—three sentences. I'm told that in Washington the veneer on the talking points is so thin that it rubs off after two.


I concur in your good opinion of Tom Paine, and I can understand why you assigned the last five pages of your presentation to the strenuous reminding of the conference participants of Paine's importance to the American Revolution. As you say, had Paine not published *Common Sense* in the winter of 1776, Jefferson six months later might not have found either the language or the occasion for the writing of the Declaration of Independence. The country inherits from Paine the boon of liberty, and I was glad to see that you cited acknowledgments of the gift from authorities as eminent as Benjamin Franklin, George Washington, Walt Whitman, and Thomas Edison.

But you didn't mention John Adams, and Adams these days is all the rage, his reputation refurbished (cf. the recent books by David McCullough and Joseph Ellis) to match the political bias currently installed in Washington. Adams saw in Paine "a little busy meddling scribbler," a foul-mouthed drunkard stirring up the Philadelphia rabble with ill-bred criticisms of privilege and wealth, an "insolent Blasphemer of things sacred and transcendent Libeller of all that is good." An attitude toward free speech, Professor, not unlike the one endorsed by Rupert Murdoch and Vice President Dick Cheney.

Adams voiced the sentiments of the Federalist Party and the country's moneyed interests, expressing what he called "my fundamental maxim of government," in the phrase "never to trust the lamb to the wolf." To Adams the lamb was property, and where today could you find a more succinct statement of the principles embraced by the Congress and approved by the Supreme Court? How better to explain the Bush Administration's approach to tax and antitrust law, to health insurance and the environment?

You conclude your remarks by exhorting the journalists of our own day to imitate the example of Paine's eloquence and courage, but you would be better advised to ask them how soon they hoped to appear with Regis Philbin on *Who Wants to Be a Millionaire*. You forget that you're talking about a news media as certain as Adams that no good can come from talking out of turn. Dissent doesn't sell, Professor; the ballet company known as the Washington press corps dances to the music of the White House Marine Band, and it will help you to better appreciate their performance if you can imagine Cokie Roberts in a tutu, or Stone Phillips as Prince Florimund leaping across the stage in a series of faultless *grand jetés*. At the ballet company's annual Gridiron Dinner three months after last year's mockery of a presidential election, the menus were printed in the form of butterfly ballots. A small bow of courtesy, you understand, a little joke for we happy few here in the ballroom of the Capital Hilton, the gesture *en pointe* meant to reassure President Bush, the evening's principal guest, that he was in hands as safe as those of the good people at Allstate.

\*     \*     \*

It isn't that the country lacks for public intellectuals, Professor, but rather that you search for them in the wrong place. You expect to find them keeping company with John Milton and Thucydides on a bookstore shelf of Penguin Classics, or somewhere in the remote but virtuous province of C-SPAN, drawing diagrams of cruise missiles or stem cells in a community-college auditorium in Duluth. Look instead to the gossip columns and the super-market press; ask around among the friends of Nicole Kidman and Sean "Puffy" Combs.

Your mistake is one in elementary grammar. Failing to grasp the proper relation between the words "public" and "intellectual," you assign too much weight to the noun, too little to the adjective. Long ago and once upon a time the display of knowledge or the proof of genius preceded the prize of fame. First write a worthwhile book and then step forward onto the stage of crowned celebrity. Now we reverse the procedure. First celebrity, then the book. Why else do you suppose that President Clinton receives $10 million to write a memoir that even his publisher knows will prove to be a long and smiling lie?

So also with every other celebrity of large magnitude. It is the fact of their success that makes them wise. Already public, they become, by definition and as a matter of commercial copyright, intellectual. We know them when we see them, not by their words or chapter headings but by their limousines and their clothes, by the crowds that attend their comings in and goings out of Spago.

Parse the phrase correctly and the country swarms with public intellectuals—Madonna speaking up for the Brazilian rain forest, Charlton Heston for the Bill of Rights; Steven Seagal unwinding the sacred scroll of Tibetan Buddhism, Tom Cruise elucidating the mystery of Scientology, Brigitte Bardot translating the secret language of dogs.

And who's to judge that what a celebrity has to say is of less consequence than what you're likely to find on the editorial pages of the *Washington Post* or the *New York Times?* Match the credentials of Sting against those of George Will or Thomas Friedman, and who comes to the microphone with a clearer view of post-modern politics or a shrewder understanding of the global economy? The odds favor the testimony of Sting, a witness more widely traveled, considerably richer, and capable of backing up his evidence with an accompaniment on electric bass.

Who better to make sense of what now constitutes the culture (the living one as opposed to the one embalmed in the Library of Congress) than the people who embody the expression of that culture's genius? Prior to the twentieth century the bulk of the world's literature was written by men who had played a part on the stage of public event. You named Sophocles and Caesar, both of them military commanders; you also might have mentioned Montaigne, Bacon, Hamilton, and Churchill, all of them politicians. Why not then Tom Brokaw or Susan Sarandon?

Regard the human intellect as a natural resource as abundant as silicon or sunlight, and you can write the story of civilization in terms of the uses to which it has been put. The seventeenth century was interested in religion and so assigned to clergymen the role of public intellectual; the eighteenth-century Enlightenment shifted the focus to politics and thus produced not only John Adams and your own Tom Paine but also Voltaire, Burke,

Napoleon, the Elder and Younger Pitt. The nineteenth century promoted scientists and novelists to the ranks of higher consciousness; our own age chooses to nominate synonyms for money—important movie stars, wealthy businessmen, musicians in heavy fur.

History grossly simplified, Professor, but I trust you to take the abbreviated point. Times change, and so does the costume of the Philosopher King. Education doesn't figure in the job description. The five speakers at your symposium brought with them the collective holding of twenty-three college degrees, and I'm sure that every one of them can spot the difference between a Beethoven piano sonata and one of Picasso's clowns. Spot it almost every time, I'll bet, the identification confirmed by deft references to Chartres Cathedral and the last Hapsburg. Solid stuff, Professor, but to what avail? You say that next year's conference will address "The Dilemma of the Creative Mind," and who do you want to see on the stage—the same five curators of the liberal-arts museum or the lead guitarist for Radiohead?

It's not your fault. The loss that you describe has been with us for fifty years, and maybe it will hearten you to know that others have looked into the same abyss. Writing a letter to his British publisher in 1949, Raymond Chandler, the author of *The Big Sleep* and *The Long Goodbye*, put it as follows:

> You can't produce art by trying, by setting up exacting standards, by talking about critical minutiae, by the Flaubert method. It is produced with great ease, in an almost offhand manner, and without self consciousness. You can't write just because you have read all the books.

Or the critic Dwight Macdonald on looking into *Life* magazine in 1960:

> Nine color pages of Renoir paintings followed by a picture of a roller-skating horse. . . . Just think, nine pages of Renoirs! But that roller-skating horse comes along, and the final impression is that Renoir is talented, but so is the horse.

For Chandler's word "art" substitute "public intellectual"; for Macdonald's horse substitute Warren Beatty and there you have an ending for your melancholy rhyme. Fortunately we don't live in times that try men's souls. Paine's rhetoric carried a ragged and starving army through a hard winter at Valley Forge; our own Washington ballet company takes up positions, *demi-pointe* and *port de bras*, pleasing to the wives of warm and well-fed oil-company lobbyists. Count your blessings, Professor; be glad that in Santa Cruz it doesn't snow.

*October 2001*

# *Wall Painting*

The artistic temperament is a disease that afflicts amateurs.
—G. K. CHESTERTON

*I*n New York last spring Christie's sold at auction, for
$26,400, an idea for a drawing. Not the drawing itself. Noth-
ing so crass as an object or a design on paper, but the right
to render the drawing in a space eight feet square. The buyer of
the work in question, *Ten Thousand Lines Ten Inches Long, Covering
the Wall Evenly*, received a sales receipt and a set of instructions
not unlike the page in a first-grade coloring book inviting a child
to connect the dots. The buyer retained the right to choose the
texture and placement of the wall—stucco, fiberboard, facing
south, in the library—but it was strongly recommended that he
hire (at his own considerable expense) the artist's own draftsmen
to draw the lines in their proper width and sequence. Under the
terms of the sale, the buyer further agreed to wash the drawing
off the wall if and when he decided to sell it to another collector
or donate it to a museum. The subsequent owner would be entitled to proof of erasure.

The artist, Sol LeWitt, expounded the thesis of conceptual art as long ago as 1969: "Ideas can be works of art—they are in a chain of development that may eventually find some form. All ideas need not be physical."

The observation is neither new nor profound. An unkind critic might go so far as to say that it was both fatuous and banal, on a par with the discovery that sailors have been known to die by drowning. But the unkind critic would miss the point and fail to appreciate LeWitt as a prophet. Within the span of a single generation LeWitt's minimalist aesthetic has come to define the character of postmodernist politics, sex, literature, and war.

For many years now the more refined literary fictions have relied on the techniques of omission. The authors tastefully leave out of their narratives all the emotion and most of the drama. In the manner of Samuel Beckett or Ann Beattie, they supply 10,000 lines of oblique irony with which the reader is expected to construct his or her own story on a blank page. Sometimes the authors furnish a few lines of dialogue, but in language so abstract that the words can mean anything the reader wishes them to mean. The effect bears comparison to a conversation partially overheard at a distance of 400 feet through the rifts in a strong wind.

What else is the presidency of Ronald Reagan if not a work of conceptual art? Like LeWitt, the president has a talent for promoting what isn't there. All his speeches, all his tinseled sentiments, all his homilies and tiny sermons might as well be entitled *Ten Thousand Words Five Letters Long, Covering the Silence Evenly*. He invites his audience to hear what they choose to hear, to connect the dots and make their own drawings of America the Beautiful.

Throughout the spring and summer the Iran-Contra committees listened to daily reports of a National Security Council gone sick with paranoid delusions of Oriental grandeur, but none of the testimony damaged Reagan's reputation as a man of benign and democratic intent. Various unkind critics wondered why so much evidence produced so small a result. Their confusion followed from their failure to understand the minimalist aesthetic.

What was important about the hearing was what wasn't said and who wasn't there. If the politicians were careful not to ask impolite questions (about Israel's percentage in the deal, or the character of the assassins and arms dealers with whom the United States allied itself in two hemispheres), the witnesses were equally careful to describe the White House and the Departments of State and Defense as large empty spaces in which nobody of importance was ever present. All of the witnesses had heard rumors about the drawing in progress (*Ten Thousand Memoranda Ten Paragraphs Long, Covering the Failure Evenly*), but none of them had ever seen it rendered on a government wall. Certainly the president hadn't seen it, and neither had Secretaries Weinberger and Shultz. The only man that everybody was sure had seen it—William Casey, former director of the CIA—was dead.

What is telephone sex if not a display of conceptual art? The Puritan bias of the American mind, strongly fortified by the fear of AIDS, has chased the nation's sexual expression into the realms of the abstract. The back pages of the better pornographic magazines glow with advertisements for "live phone fantasy," "mind images," "telefantasies," "sensuous, exotic, live phone playmates!"

In return for a draftsman's fee (all major credit cards accepted), Lori or Cherry Blossom or Evita agree to describe any number of erotic acts ("150 Portrayals; Safe and Private!") that might be entitled *Ten Thousand Whispers One Syllable Long, Covering the Night Evenly*. To render the promises in physical form might prove too expensive, too inconvenient, too dangerous.

The curators of the nation's foreign policy haven't yet learned to manage their affairs as efficiently as Lori or Evita, but certainly they think of their wars and stratagems as works of conceptual art. The current naval expedition into the Persian Gulf might well be entitled *Ten Thousand Radar Signals Ten Seconds Long, Covering the Map Evenly*. The Reagan Administration apparently wishes to make an avant-garde statement about America's place and stature in the world. To what end, or at what cost, nobody can say. Our geopoliticians don't know what the United States stands to win or lose in the event of a war with Iran, Iraq, or any other enemy as yet unannounced, but clearly the excitements of the moment demand something impressive in "a chain of development that may eventually find some form." Understood as objects as crass as a collection of ungainly ships in warm water, our fleet has little or no chance of victory within the confines of what amounts to an Iranian lake. Understood as minimalist art, as an idea of power rather than a fact of power, our navy is invincible. We supply the military schematics and expect our enemies to fill in the blanks with their own trembling and fear.

LeWitt's drawing was one of the first works of conceptual art to be sold at auction, but I expect the prices to move steadily

higher. The trend is so well established that the leading Democratic candidate for the 1988 presidential nomination exists as a
set of instructions for a series of yet unconnected dots. Mario
Cuomo retains his value in the opinion polls precisely because he
hasn't declared his candidacy, because the political consultants
(i.e., the analogues of LeWitt's draftsmen and the girls on "Lori's
Hotline") haven't drawn his 10,000 lines on the walls of the
media.

If the trend continues to follow the ascent of the stock market
and the price of New York real estate, maybe the public will learn
to occupy impalpable states of theory and possibility. Give people
enough practice with the aesthetic, and maybe they will be persuaded to omit the tiresome chore of having to live their lives.
Museums like to collect conceptual art because it takes up so little
space in the basement. Rapacious landlords and ambitious politicians like to collect conceptual lives because they make so few
demands and such little noise.

*October 1987*

# Capitalist Tool

In democracies, nothing is greater or more brilliant than
commerce. It attracts the attention of the public and fills the
imagination of the multitude.
—ALEXIS DE TOCQUEVILLE

When I listen to Steve Forbes make political speeches,
I think of my Great-aunt Evelyn, who, at the age of
sixty-three, took up a career as an opera singer. Nobody in the family ever understood why she did so, but she was
a woman of substantial wealth and impervious to suggestions (very
hesitant and modest suggestions) that she possessed no talent for
her chosen art. Her whims descended upon her in sudden gusts
of inspiration, and one summer afternoon, without prior warning
or explanation, she installed on her estate in Connecticut a maestro
imported from the basement at La Scala. For the next eighteen
months, wandering through the halls of the house in which the
servants fled the sound of her approach, she practiced her scales
and trills and sang, in a wavering mezzo-soprano voice, the arias
of Giacomo Puccini and Christoph Willibald Gluck. When the

maestro pronounced her the equal of Renata Tebaldi, she hired
Town Hall for her New York debut. The performance wasn't as
well attended as Forbes's progress through the New Hampshire
snow, but what the audience lacked in size and camera equipment,
it made up for with the fervor of buoyant expectations that filled
the first five rows of an otherwise empty auditorium. Aunt Evelyn
was no fool, and she had taken the precaution of informing her
friends, relatives, and dependents that anybody marked absent for
the evening would be omitted from her will.

The concert lasted nearly three hours, without what the Italian
maestro regarded as the indulgence of an intermission. Holding
herself firmly erect in front of the grand piano, wearing a black
dress and a necklace suggestive of ancient Egyptian royalty, Aunt
Evelyn brought forth her entire repertoire (arranged in historical
order from operas of Monteverdi to those of Richard Wagner), and
never once did she sing five consecutive notes in the same key.
Every now and then she made an inexplicably abrupt and impe-
rious gesture with the palm frond that served as her only prop.

Forbes displayed a similar awkwardness in front of the C-SPAN
cameras, but his determination was as unblinking as Aunt Evelyn's, and so was his serene indifference to the prospect of ridicule.
Although obviously unfamiliar with public places and uneasy in
crowds, he was a man so seized by the glory of the flat tax that
he bravely endured what he called "the hazing of the American
political system" and stoically ignored the reports of his campaign
having foundered on the shoals of the Iowa caucuses. Watching
him exhibit his collection of reactionary economic theory (not only
the flat tax but also the return to the gold standard, the long-lost

Laffer curve, and the maxims of Friedrich von Hayek), I thought of an amiably myopic British peer earnestly showing the weekend guests his prize poultry, and I couldn't see in him the character of vile usurper preferred by his rival candidates and a quorum of the country's important newspaper columnists. The invective of Senator Bob Dole I could ascribe to the envy of a politician unendowed with limitless supplies of money, but the press criticism had about it an air of churlish ingratitude.

Here was an affable and well-intentioned citizen, furiously riding his hobbyhorse around a course of New England shopping malls, providing, at his own not inconsiderable expense, a civic entertainment meant to teach a lesson in the noble art of American self-government. So many and so generous were the gifts of his campaign that none of the attending journalists lacked occasion for a witticism or a sermon. The humorists compared him to a glass owl, a bobbing-head doll in the back of a car, a giant white rabbit, a toy robot, and an enameled Easter egg; the moralists pointed to his presumption as proof that money had so besmudged the polished brightwork of the American political machinery that the presidency had become an office as easily bought as a municipal judgeship or a seat in the United States Senate. Nobody had the grace to say that the candidate and his money might have wandered off into less public-spirited directions, that while Forbes was pursuing his political pastime in New Hampshire, John Eleuthère du Pont (the heir to another magnificent American fortune) lost one of the Olympic wrestlers whom he had been tending like a flock of merino sheep on his estate in suburban Pennsylvania.

*       *       *

Wealth in sufficient measure grants its possessors the right to their enthusiasms, and if they can afford to rent a concert hall or hire Johnnie Cochran, on what ground is it possible to quarrel with the dreams of self projected in the mirrors of the news? More often than not the equestrian classes occupy themselves with animals and architecture (Aaron Spelling's house in Westwood, the late Doris Duke's pet camels, etc.), but a certain kind of rich man prefers the pleasures of moral or political dandyism. He feels obliged to hold views, espouse causes, restore order. The spectacle is nearly always comic—H. Ross Perot as a latter-day Oliver Cromwell, Michael Huffington come to rescue California from the sin of pride, Donald Trump at the zenith of his celebrity in the middle 1980s buying full-page advertisements in the *New York Times* to explain his thinking about Japan; Mortimer Zuckerman acquiring *U.S. News & World Report* for $185 million (a sum nearly double that of the going rate for the presidency) in order to appoint himself resident sage as well as editor in chief. Most newly arrived publishers at least have the wit to regard their property as a kind of very expensive rubber duck, and they content themselves with giving lunches for wandering dignitaries and deciding the broad questions of national policy. Zuckerman had it in mind to make a grander entrance into the intellectual limelight. Week after week, traveling to Moscow before the Geneva Summit Conference or to Manila just after the revolution, he returned with breathless discoveries of the obvious—"Readiness for war is part of the problem as well as part of the solution," or, more urgently, "Pre-emptive surrender is not good negotiating doctrine."

What was remarkable about the Forbes campaign was neither the candidate's vanity nor his tendency to speak of himself in the third person, but the willing suspensions of disbelief granted both to his impersonation of a populist and his promise of a new economic dawn. Striking the two poses simultaneously—the sudden lurching of his left hand uncannily reminiscent of Aunt Evelyn's palm frond—Forbes stood before his fairground audiences in Manchester or Concord as a friend of the common man, threatening to "drive a stake through [the] heart" of the tax code, railing against the corrupt "lackeys" and "politicians" in Washington who were forever milking the elk of honest American labor.

It was an earnest speech and undoubtedly heartfelt, but it belonged, like Aunt Evelyn's opera singing, to the surrealist school of public declamation. The system that Forbes denounced was the one to which he owed his fortune and his boyish grin—the system under which he pays an annual property tax of $2,111 on a 520-acre farm in Bedminster, New Jersey, and sets the price of a weekend's political jaunt at a sum equivalent to what most everybody else in his democratic audience could expect to earn in a year. Forbes improved upon the surrealistic effect by proposing as a remedy for the country's economic distress precisely those measures that under the direction of the Reagan Administration had run the annual deficit from $79 billion in 1981 to $290 billion in 1992—i.e., a bankrupt economic theory dressed up with a new set of feathers (eliminating all deductions and taxes on interest, pensions, dividends, inheritance and capital gains) certain to vastly enhance the wealth and power of a grasping plutocracy from which the candidate in the expensive blue suit promised to retrieve the ladies and gentlemen wearing quilted parkas and bomber jackets.

But no tumultous questions drifted forward to the podium and no angry voice rose up in the back row of the gym. The silence was respectful, the shaking of the candidate's hand as reverent as the kissing of a cardinal's ring. I thought of Aunt Evelyn coming mercifully to the end of her first concert, the audience rising to its feet in a storm of tumultuous applause, and the cries of "Brava" echoing through the empty hall. The accompanist bowed deeply before the wonder of the diva's art. A destitute nephew presented a bouquet of roses for which he had pawned his watch. A threadbare niece was heard to remark that never before had she understood the importance of Gluck.

Admiring Forbes's repeated escapes from the mockery of his imagined peers, it occurred to me that he owed his standing in the opinion polls not simply to the sum of money that he had paid for his campaign (some $14 million in the last three months of 1995, $6 million in the first six weeks of 1996), nor even to the sunny optimism of his prerecorded message about the "spiritual renewal" and "economic boom" awaiting his fellow countrymen over the horizon of the next election, but to his personification of the American dream. When a man as rich as Forbes stands revealed in the full glory of a net worth of $439 million, it is as if Mammon himself had stepped off the bus from Portsmouth.

America is a nation of expectant capitalists, all of us hoping to join the company of the monied immortals who can play at being gods and do anything they wish—drive fast cars, charter four-masted sailing vessels, produce movies, drink the wine of orgy, and campaign for political office—and here at last was a man who had drawn the winning number in the lottery of birth.

Word of Forbes's fortune preceded him like a brass band or a pillar of fire. The media were careful to confine their jokes and moralisms to the editorial page; the front-page stories preferred to inventory the candidate's store of earthly treasure—a palace in Tangier, the estate in New Jersey decorated with the picturesque comings and goings of the Essex Fox Hounds and the Tewksbury Foot Bassetts, houses in New York and London, an art collection, a château in France, a mountain in Colorado, an island in Tahiti. Best and most wonderful of all, Forbes himself was so untroubled by the worries of ordinary men that when asked by the *Wall Street Journal* to reflect on the trials and obstacles of his life, he was hard put to remember any. Working backwards in time past the memory of inheriting his father's magazine and his incarnation as a Princeton student, he came at last to his leaving home for a New England prep school, a challenging adventure that had taught him, he said, "why pioneers went out."

Because Forbes's fortune had come to him from the divine cloud that also had descended upon the Mellons and the du Ponts, it wouldn't have mattered if he had been made of tin or carved in wood. Like Presidents Kennedy and Reagan, the candidate had about him an air of reassuring opulence, a little stiff perhaps and overly pleased with his own escapade, but familiar with the comforts of the safer suburbs and knowing that it is the lot of the successful American politician to put a smiling face on the imperatives of property.

As I watched Forbes blandly turn aside the questions asked of him by Ted Koppel and Larry King, I remembered not only Aunt Evelyn's concert but the Senate Rules Committee in the autumn of 1974 questioning Nelson Rockefeller about his fitness for the vice presidency of the United States. Rockefeller had been appointed to that office by President Gerald Ford, and in full view of a nation still alarmed by Richard Nixon's betrayal of the public trust, not a single senator could bring himself to ask a hard question. Overcome with awe in the presence of Rockefeller's fortune, even the skeptics on the committee prostrated themselves before the witness like slaves staring into Pharaoh's golden face.

The complex mechanisms of the modern world depend as certainly on the faith in money as the structures of the medieval world depended on the faith in God. To the extent that the society employs an intrinsically worthless medium of exchange—paper or numbers on a screen instead of gold or land or furs—the expansion of its wealth demands increasingly daring suspensions of disbelief. The flesh becomes word, and the numbers come together in poetic metaphors. Make the numbers big enough, and then make them immanent in all the world's credit cards, and people will believe almost anything—even Steve Forbes dressed up as a populist or the promise of a happy return to the good old days in America when nobody, not even Andrew Carnegie, was forced to swallow the insult of an income tax.

The newspaper columnists who worried about what was to become of Thomas Jefferson's republic and Andrew Jackson's democracy in an age of virtual reality wrote testy editorials about the American presidency being sold at auction to any rich sportsman with a taste for summit conferences instead of polo ponies. Their fretting seemed to me as vain as their complaints about Forbes's lack of a public record. No man ever comes to the White House with sufficient wisdom or experience, and unless we change the campaign finance laws—allowing individual citizens to contribute a good deal more than $1,000 to candidates whom they admire—who else except the very rich can afford the costs of the television promotions while at the same time keeping up the appearance of moral virtue and independent mind?

The entrance onto the national political stage of so many wealthy amateurs suggests that the holding of public office has become largely ceremonial—a matter of knowing which fork to select at a state dinner, when to smile and how to read a script, where to stand for the photo op, and how to present to the American people an image of dignity and calm. Given our American belief that money is the alpha and omega of human existence and the god from which all blessings flow, who better to serve as Pontifex Maximus and chief priest of the American civil religion than a figure already encased in gold?

As herald of the opulent new morning in America, Forbes is probably too early in the field to win the prize of the White

House. Like Aunt Evelyn, who abandoned her concert career after three seasons and five voice teachers, he presumably will discover other means of expressing his concern for his fellow man. Aunt Evelyn devoted the latter part of her life to the growing of geraniums, and maybe Forbes will take up the collecting of butterflies or stamps.

*April 1996*

# Back to School

Ambition hath no mean, it is either upon all fours
or upon tiptoes.
—MARQUIS OF HALIFAX

*I*n early July I noticed a story in the *New York Times* about college professors at Amherst and Wesleyan dressing up their lecture courses with titles meant to draw a crowd—"Great Hits of Medieval Literature," "The Souls of Animals," "For Every Pharaoh There Is a Moses"—and I cut the page from the paper with the thought of writing an essay about the classical curriculum fitted to the wheel of progress and pressed into the mold of commercial trend. Two days later, before I had assembled even the beginning of an idea, I received a letter from H. J. Whitaker, a professor of English at a university in southern New England whom I had presumed safely immured in the research for his long-promised book on the Earl of Oxford. His letter rendered superfluous any commentary that I might have had in mind, but as with most of the news these days from the academic frontiers it requires a word of introduction.

Not having seen or heard from Whitaker in three years, I remembered him as a gray and bookish man obsessively preoccupied
with the spectacle of the sixteenth century, a scholar fond of footnotes, lutes, and puns. But I also knew that he possessed an antic
sense of humor, much refined by his study of the Elizabethan wits,
and that if his circumstances had been somewhat different, he
might have found his way onto the stage of *Saturday Night Live*.
Apparently it was his gift for comedy that got him into trouble.
When the chairman of the History Department fell suddenly ill
last winter, Whitaker was asked to provide a spring-semester
course that satisfied the requirements in both the history and
humanities majors. "Nothing difficult," he said in his letter.
"Nothing more than a few lectures sufficient to amuse the grad-
uating seniors during their final season under the elm trees and
to furnish the slow-witted among them with the last of their
necessary credits."

The department didn't care what he taught, and because he
happened to be re-reading Castiglione's *Book of the Courtier*, the
principal Renaissance treatise on the staging of self-promotions,
it occurred to him to teach the dance of grace and favor as performed by the ladies and gentlemen attending the magnificence
of Lorenzo de' Medici and Elizabeth I. He had noticed that his
students spent much of their time making connections and net-
working their address books ("grooming their résumés like show
dogs"), and he thought they might enjoy knowing that their anx-
ieties were as old as Hampton Court.

The dean objected to the proposition on the ground that it

lacked "relevance," and before Whitaker knew what he was saying and without taking thought of the consequences, he shifted his *mise en scène* to the contemporary United States and set off on a manic improvisation aping and commenting upon the abject displays of flattery practiced not only by Washington politicians but also by the New York literary crowd, the grandees of the country's larger business corporations, and the hangers-on thriving like California mushrooms in the shadow of Steven Spielberg or Sharon Stone.

The dean was enchanted. Whitaker tried to disavow the performance, explaining that he had never met Spielberg or Stone (let alone Hillary Clinton or Salman Rushdie) and that he knew a good deal more about Shakespeare's Globe Theater than he did about Hollywood restaurants or the game of musical chairs in the executive offices of IBM and Time Warner. But the dean, a literal-minded man and desperate for enrollment, was already on the phone with the registrar.

"Never attempt a joke in the presence of a college administrator," Whitaker said. "Not unless it results in a gift to the library."

Attendance bore out the dean's sense of the market, and by the third week in April the classroom had become so crowded that late-arriving students were forced to stand in the hall or look in through the mullioned windows. The provost dropped by for the lecture on "The Trap of Friendship," which impressed him as a proof of the university's "commitment to the cutting edge of the twenty-first century," and on the Monday after Commencement the dean ordered Whitaker to prepare a full-year course under the title "The American Courtier: The Great Tradition." Offering the use of the Law School auditorium and the services of four research assistants, the dean clapped Whitaker on the back and told him that he was on his way to the academic limelight.

Whitaker didn't know whether he welcomed or dreaded the prospect. Although pleased by his newfound glory, he was nervous about both the size of the audience (the dean had mentioned upwards of 300 students) and the nature of the instruction (vocational instead of avocational), and because he was a diligent scholar, he knew that he hadn't done enough reading. The standard texts were obvious enough—Castiglione, La Bruyère's *Characters*, Saint-Simon's memoirs, Oscar Wilde's plays and aphorisms—but as he began searching the American sources he was astonished to discover that the Americans were even more assiduous than the Renaissance Italians in their cultivation of the garden of welcome lies. The literature was vast, in periodicals as well as books, consisting of self-help manuals, White House memoirs, celebrity confessions, and muckraking journalism, and the historical precedents were as unmistakable as the Washington Monument.

"Consider closely the lives of our great men," Whitaker said, "and who do we find beneath the surfaces of noble marble? True and worthy ancestors of our own beloved Bill Moyers and Barbara Walters."

Reading about the rules of self-advancement in Philadelphia in 1763, Whitaker had found Benjamin Franklin courting the favor of influential patrons, striking the pose of "the Humble Enquirer," preaching the virtues of calculation and civility, even writing verses in praise of caution, prudence, and coldness of heart—e.g., "The weakest Foe boasts some revenging Pow'r; The weakest Friend some serviceable Hour."

On the western frontier in 1831 Whitaker came across Alexis de Tocqueville passing through Nashville and Cincinnati and noticing that although the Americans didn't dress as well or as expensively as the ladies and gentlemen in France, they possessed a native talent for ingratiating themselves with anybody and everybody who could do them a service or grant them a privilege. Dandies in broadcloth instead of silk brocade, Whitaker said, loud in their brag and fantastic in their gestures, bowing and scraping in front of one another while standing up to their ankles in the muddy street of a wooden town.

But nothing had taken Whitaker more by surprise than the Horatio Alger stories. "I had expected street urchins rising from rags to riches by dint of their hard work and noble character. Not at all. The Tattered Toms and Ragged Dicks succeed because they happen to be standing in the right place at the right time, encountering by accident a benign plutocrat for whom they play the part of dutiful and obliging son and so inherit the fortune."

Overwhelmed by the surfeit of sources, and knowing that he couldn't master all the variants of his topic within the time at hand, Whitaker still hoped to avoid making a fool of himself (especially if the child of somebody famous chanced to be sitting in the third row), and his apprehension brought him to the purpose of his letter. Enclosing the outline of lectures for the fall term, together with the synopsis that he had written for the college catalogue, he asked me to make any revisions that came to mind and encouraged me to show the syllabus to anybody else who might suggest improvements. I take the sentence to mean that he wouldn't mind seeing some of its finer passages in print.

## CATALOGUE COPY

### History 420: THE AMERICAN COURTIER

An examination of the means of personal self-advancement from the American Revolution to the present. Particular emphasis on the degrees of calculation necessary for a successful career in business, politics, or the arts.

Prerequisite: History 121 or the equivalent. Readings in Castiglione, Shakespeare, Saint-Simon, Talleyrand, Franklin, Wilde, Kissinger, Bradlee, Clinton, Liz Smith.

MWF/1:30–2:20 Cr/year only

#### COURSE OF STUDY FALL TERM

*Week 1—The Courtier as the Hero of Our Time*

1) Discarding negative stereotypes and correcting false impressions.

2) The courtier not to be confused with the toady, the suck-up, the lick-spittle, or the brown-nose (Castiglione, Diderot, Bob Woodward, Larry King).

3) Prostitution an honorable profession (Selected readings: the *Wall Street Journal*'s editorial page).

*Week 3—Opinions*

1) The safety of platitudes: candor always a mistake.

2) Successful topics of conversation—sports, birds, foreigners, gardens, movie stars, zoos, money.

3) Ignorance a blessing; fitting an opinion to the color of the drapes; the art of saying absolutely nothing (*Foreign Affairs, The American Spectator*).

*Week 6—Striking Poses*

1) The importance of being seen, especially in the company of people more celebrated than oneself (*People*, assorted gossip columnists).

2) Politics compared to fashion photography; the poses of Senator Alfonse D'Amato likened to those of Cindy Crawford.

3) Which books and moral certainties to bring to literary conferences; whether to play tennis or go on the rafting trip; learning to think of oneself as an expensive suit.

*Week 9—Flattery*

1) Why there never can be too much of it (biographies of Lee Iacocca and Alexander Haig).

2) The seven degrees of the servile smile (videotape, ABC News—Jennings, Donaldson, Walters).

3) Fulsome compliments and congratulatory notes (the collected letters of Bill Clinton and George Bush).

*Week 10—The Trap of Friendship*

1) A friend a foolish luxury. Loyalty not a virtue.

2) The distinction between a friend and a connection. The glance sinister and the cut direct.

3) The timely betrayal (Kissinger, Nixon, et al.).

*Week 12—Appearances, Their Sovereign Rule*
1) It is only shallow people who do not judge by appearances. Knowledge differentiated from knowingness. Showing credibility and resolve.

2) Perception management; cosmetic surgery; shoes and hats.

3) The perfect courtier (Colin Powell, Diane Sawyer).

On reading Whitaker's notes for the second time, I could see him warming to his theme, persuaded of its seriousness by the force of his own rhetoric, and I wondered why Yale and Harvard hadn't thought to offer a similar course of study. Certainly the character of the unctuous careerist was as familiar in faculty common rooms as in Washington policy institutes and Hollywood television studios, and why not present the character as an admirable one? Why not, in Whitaker's phrase, "put an end to the old Puritan superstitions about the wickedness of silk and Charles II"?

Caught up in the excitement of transferring his preoccupation with Elizabethan etiquette to the protocols of late-twentieth-century American wealth and celebrity, Whitaker was offended by our own latter-day media, "both news and entertainment divisions," continuing the program of moralizing sermons about the American hero as a voice of conscience, forever crying in the wilderness, standing on a principled soapbox to announce, usually to a crowd of seven, a bitter or eternal truth. "What rot!" he said.

"The pieties ignore the facts." What else is the courtier spirit, he said, if not the spirit of a society overrun by lawyers? A lawyer, like any journalist or actor, is by definition a courtier hired to arrange the truth in its most flattering and convenient poses, a smiling and accommodating person loyal to power under whatever name it presents itself, constructing the edifice of a brilliant career by saying to a succession of masters: Make of me what you want; I am what you want me to be.

Roused to the point of righteous indignation, Whitaker asked a prosecutor's question: "Isn't this the attitude that corporations expect of their junior executives, or campaign managers of their candidates, or women of their dogs?" His studies had convinced him that the courtier spirit is far more necessary to a democracy than to a monarchy. The figure of the prince wears so many faces (network executive, town clerk, syndicated columnist) that a democracy transforms the relatively few favors in a monarch's gift (sinecure, benefice, patents royal) into the vast supply of grace and favor distributed under the rubrics of tax exemption, defense contract, publication, milk subsidy, tenure. Courts form like oyster shells not only around the pearls of great price at IBM and the Walt Disney Company but also around Oprah Winfrey and Wayne Gretzky. Once instructed in the correct forms of agreeable behavior and expedient speech, the ambitious careerist in attendance at one court finds it a simple matter to perform the same services for other well-placed patrons in other well-furnished rooms.

Which presumably is why Whitaker's dean booked him into the Law School auditorium. If the reports in the newspapers can be believed, college students these days think that if they miss their first and maybe only chance at the brass ring, they might never find their way home to the putting greens of Fairfield County or the music on the beach of Malibu. Well aware that they have little choice but to become dependent upon a corporate overlord (not only for wages but for the terms of their existence, for pension, medical insurance, club membership, and definition of self), how could they not want to learn the ways and means of keeping their places in the sun? Another three semesters in the academic limelight, and I can imagine Whitaker, sometimes on tiptoes but more often on all fours, addressing business conventions, developing projects for PBS, lecturing at the Kennedy School of Government.

*September 1996*

# Balzac's Garret

Heard melodies are sweet, but those unheard
Are sweeter; therefore, ye soft pipes, play on.
—JOHN KEATS, "ODE ON A GRECIAN URN"

As a poor and unpublished writer in Paris in the early 1820s, Honoré de Balzac lived in a meager garret under a roof of broken tiles near the cemetery of Père Lachaise. The landlord provided nothing other than a table, a bed, and a chair, and so Balzac, who was fond of luxury, dressed the room in words. On a stained and empty wall he inscribed the notice "Rosewood paneling with commode"; on the opposite wall, equally bare, "Gobelin tapestry with Venetian mirror"; and in the place of honor over the cold fireplace, "Picture by Raphael." Twenty years later, having become both famous and rich, Balzac filled his several apartments and townhouses with the literal-minded proofs of his once impoverished hypothesis—mirrors both Venetian and French, Sèvres porcelain, picture by Delacroix.

The progression from fantastic wish to literal fact followed the plot of what until recently would have been recognized as a standard American success—young man of promise storms the walls of the capital city, climbs the ladder of ambition, gives weight and form to the images of his desire, makes his way across the dance floor of the best society, and achieves the stature of a commodity. The story is no longer so standard, and if I can believe what I read in the papers about the numbers of people whose economic well-being has been eliminated or much reduced, the line of the narrative has turned back on itself—middle-aged pillar of the community falls through the trapdoor of an unforeseen merger, descends the stair of humiliation, withdraws to a garden apartment near a suburban freeway, and there contents himself with the heartening or poetic notices posted on the Internet.

The friends of the new global economic order haven't yet gotten around to promoting the changed direction of the American journey—away from the fertile plain of well-watered department stores and into the desert of metaphysics—but they make a solemn show of worrying about what's to become of the once-prosperous American middle class, and in another two or three years I expect that we will begin to see the travel posters: COME TO THE LAND OF MAKE-BELIEVE. TAKE HEART IN THE THINGS OF THE SPIRIT. REJOICE IN WHAT ISN'T THERE.

The good news should prove easy to sell. The longing for the ineffable and the unseen has been characteristic of the American mind since the beginning—as present in the seventeenth-century Puritan settlements on Massachusetts Bay as among the pilgrims moving west across the trans-Mississippi frontier in the 1840s or departing for Paris in the 1920s to join the legion of the lost generation—and it is a mistake to think of the Americans as a materialist people. Foreign or leftist observers like to imagine the United States as a caricature of a nineteenth-century plutocrat, an obese gentleman in a waistcoat and top hat devouring the fruits of honest labor as if they were truffles in the mouth of a pig. The emphasis on earthly appetite misses the point, and the critics who deplore the rapacious American consumption of superfluous goods fail to notice that more often than not the material acquisitions serve as tickets of admission to the desired states of immateriality. The taste of the truffle matters less than what the eating of the truffle represents—i.e., induction into the company of the elect and a place at the table of self-esteem.

We are a people captivated by the power and romance of metaphor, forever seeking the invisible through the imagery of the visible. Even if we assemble what the world is pleased to acknowledge as a fortune, we discover that it fails to satisfy the hunger of our spiritual expectation. As Tocqueville long ago noticed, "The Americans clutch everything but hold nothing fast, and lose grip as they hurry after some new delight," which explains why we never get quite all the way to the end of the American dream and accounts for the feeling of vague melancholy that echoes like a blues rhythm through the back rooms of so many American success stories.

Other than to people seeking to prove or grasp what isn't there, to whom does Pat Buchanan present his nostalgic tent-show pageant of America the Beautiful or Senator Alfonse D'Amato the congressional excitements of the Whitewater investigation? As of early March, the Senate search for swindlers and dance-hall girls on the upper reaches of the Whitewater River had run a course

of 300 days (the longest hearings ever held by the U.S. Congress
and a good deal more extensive than either the Watergate or Iran-
Contra hearings), produced 45,000 documents and 132 witnesses,
and still had failed to discover a single proof of wrongdoing on
the part of either President or Hillary Clinton. Attempting to
replicate the heroics of Teddy Roosevelt, Buchanan manages the
bravado of General George A. Custer, but his pose is no more or
less absurd than that of Colin Powell (a supple careerist and bureaucratic courtier) as a statesman of independent mind, or that
of H. Ross Perot (who made his fortune as a government contrac-
tor) as a populist come against the corruptions of Washington.
The painted melodrama is traditional, but without an audience of
born metaphysicians the Hollywood movie studios wouldn't have
become the eighth wonder of an admiring world and no American
political campaign could move its circus wagon to the next town
or the next opinion poll.

The land of make-believe has been well mapped by four gen-
erations of advertising copywriters, and as they have improved
their knowledge of the terrain, so have they learned that it is the
naming rather than the making of a thing that draws a crowd.
They sell the symbols of happiness or immortality at the counters
of abstraction, and the slogan, the designer label, the celebrity
endorsement, and the corporate trademark come to embody not
only the immortal soul of a product but also almost the entire
sum of its commercial worth. Just as the unheard melodies of
Keats's Grecian urn fill out the implied harmonies of American
politics, so also they stock the better stores and shopping malls
with celebrated brand names disguised as skirts or shoes or shav-

ing cream. At the higher elevations of abstraction, both word and image need refer to nothing other than themselves. Ringo Starr, formerly drummer to the Beatles, received $1 million from a Japanese advertising agency last winter merely to state his name in a beer commercial, and when Michael Jordan announced his return to the Chicago Bulls in 1995, share prices of the five corporations for which he serves as pitchman (among them McDonald's, Nike, and Gatorade) gained a combined value of $1 billion on the New York Stock Exchange. Sometimes, of course, symbolism fails, and what the Lord giveth, the Lord taketh away. Random House agreed to pay Joan Collins $4 million to write a novel that it reclassified as worthless drivel when she delivered the manuscript three years later—not because the visible text was anything other than expected but because its invisible subtext had blown away with the soap bubble of her fame.

As commodities increasingly come to consist of little else except information, even the sensual pleasures of the flesh drift off into the spheres of abstraction. Adulterous love affairs take place in cyberspace, and the brothels reconfigure their displays of sexual temptation as a suite of voices talking on a telephone. The going rates at the better resort hotels have less to do with the view of the mountains or the sea than with the soft pipes of flattery playing in the golf shop or the spa; the managers of expensive restaurants give more thought to the composing of the menu than to the cooking of the trout. The Chicago Board of Trade sells options on next summer's hurricanes, and baseball teams sign contracts for $10 and $20 million with stumbling outfielders unlikely to hit better than .250 in the hope that so expensive an advertisement for an imaginary prowess will bring fans to the ballpark and quickness to the player's bat. Books on spiritual or inspirational themes, often told in the voices of angels, sell far more copies than books written by even the most renowned secular humanist. Within the last two or three years the authors of pulp fiction have discovered what is known as "the Christian thriller," and Pat Robertson, founder of the Christian Coalition and once-upon-a-time candidate for president, published a novel in the form last summer under the title *The End of the Age*, in which his hero describes the events preliminary to the second coming of Christ, among them a meteor falling on Los Angeles and the Antichrist at large in the White House. The novel sold 275,000 copies.

Like the evangelist and the retail merchant, the politician and the bond-market tout seek to endow information with the character of a tangible commodity, and their art, which is a literary one, consists in persuading the faithful to see visions not unlike those vouchsafed to the early Christian saints. Year after year the country's most eminent economists make predictions consistently ridiculed by events; year after year the brokerage firms sell hundreds of millions of shares in companies that go nowhere but south; year after year the editors of investment newsletters charge handsome fees for advice that is as worthless as the geopolitical theory published in the policy journals. Nobody minds because it is understood that the learned gentlemen speak and write an unintelligible language not unlike church Latin, and in the meantime the Dow Jones average continues to rise because the customers hear the unheard dance music on the painted surface of a stockbroker's reassuring smile.

*    *    *

Given both the transcendental bias of the American mind and the genius of modern communications technology, I expect that in the not too distant future we can look forward, in Max Frisch's phrase, to "arranging the world so that we don't have to experience it." If it is true, as Marshall McLuhan suspected, that "travel now differs very little from going to a movie or turning the pages of a magazine," then we never come to any new place, and to the extent that we live within the little rooms of the electronic media (i.e., in Balzac's garret) everything becomes a name posted on a wall, a Web site, or a television screen. The habit of abstraction would explain not only Ralph Lauren's fortune and Pat Buchanan's presidential campaign but also the state of disrepair into which the United States has let fall its highways, its schools, its railroads, its cities and public squares. If the media are nothing more than the means of storing and transporting information, and if by assuming the character of information, commodities can be moved by fiber optics, fax machines, and ATM cards, then why bother to maintain an infrastructure made to the specifications of medieval Europe or ancient Rome?

Or why go to the trouble of preserving the logistics of a consumer society that depends on the moving of so many cumbersome goods that the once-prosperous American middle classes no longer can afford to buy? It is both easier and cheaper to deliver the image of a thing instead of the thing itself, and the substitution of the lighter for the heavier object conforms to the fashionable trend of the times—in line not only with the downsizing of corpulent business corporations but also with the passions for fat-free diets, the ascetic doctrines of the Eastern religions, portable offices, clothes designed to express the look of stylish poverty, and the aesthetics of minimalist art. Let enough people learn to regard the acts of reduced consumption as attenuated, postmodern forms of the full-blooded pagan ritual of getting and spending once practiced by their forefathers in the Christmas-tree forests of the 1950s, and maybe they will come to know that even the smallest bottle of perfume from Versace or Dior contains within it the dread and ancient spirit of Mammon, in much the same way that the dry crust of the Communion wafer embodies the flesh of Christ.

As Americans we make of the sermon, the sales pitch, and the lawsuit our principal forms of literary expression, and I don't doubt that the next generation of the avant-garde will prove itself capable of redefining the notion of property. Microsoft already owns electronic rights to works by Rembrandt and Da Vinci as well as those by Raphael and Delacroix, and in the newspaper a few years ago I noticed that a lawyer arguing a case about a shipwreck off the coast of South Carolina had hit upon the principles of "tele-possession" and "tele-presence." If I understand the theory correctly, it might be possible to carry the feasts of consumption into the realm of the surreal. The SS *Central America*, on a voyage from San Francisco to New York in 1857, sank in a hurricane with a cargo of gold, and the submersible robot sent by a syndicate of latter-day prospectors to search the wreck at a depth of 8,000 feet returned with photographs offered by the syndicates as proof of title. To the best of my knowledge the case is still making its way through the courts, but if the principle of tele-possession is eventually upheld, who then owns Elizabeth Taylor or the Empire State Building?

To citizens of eighteenth-century Paris too poor to buy bread, Marie Antoinette offered the famous suggestion of eating cake. Her counterparts in the palaces of late-twentieth-century capitalism—relying on what I'm told are the wonders of interactive media—might suggest the eating of pictures of cake. Even now, at almost any hour of the day or night, the cable television networks offer a buffet of food and cooking programs, many of them watched in lieu of chocolate by women on a diet, and the manufacturers of jogging shoes sell 70 percent of their product to people who don't jog.

The larger task of redirecting the American journey back from the kingdom of literal fact to the provinces of fantastic wish I expect to proceed along more or less the same lines as a presidential election campaign. Although the candidates travel around the country presenting themselves for photographs in the midst of cheering crowds, in effect they stand in an empty television studio under a ceiling of acoustic tiles. The corporate overlord provides a table, a camera, and a chair, and the authors hired for the occasion dress the room in words. On one of the blank walls they inscribe the notice, "Speedboat with gold fittings"; on the opposite wall, "California vineyard with movie star"; and, in the place of honor, behind the candidate's head, "Pictures by Walt Disney."

*May 1996*

# Traveler's Tale

All things are artificial, for nature is the art of God.
—Sir Thomas Browne

*T*hree days before Christmas last year, on an afternoon train from New Haven to New York, I found myself sitting opposite a woebegone young man in his late twenties who seemed so alarmed by the direction of his own thoughts that I was reluctant to unsettle him further with a careless remark about Newt Gingrich or the weather. I took him to be a student in one of the Yale graduate schools, but by his appearance I couldn't guess at the topic of either his dissertation or his unhappiness. He was wearing blue jeans, a worn but once well-tailored overcoat and the remnant of a gray cashmere sweater. His round and naturally pleasant face was gaunt and drawn, and although the melancholy expression in his eyes suggested the possibility of an unpublished poet, he could just as easily have been studying law or architecture.

We were among the few passengers in an unheated car, and during the first twenty minutes of the journey he stared absently out the window at the rain, his hands thrust dejectedly into the pockets of his coat. When at last he chose to speak, he didn't turn his head. The obliqueness of the statement surprised me less than its hollow tone.

"You know, of course," he said, "what they can do to mice."

I didn't know—either which they or what mice—but I understood that my companion had been asking himself a series of questions for which he had found no good answers and that his observation followed from a dismal line of reasoning that he no longer could suppress.

"It's Christmas," I said. "The end of the year. The *fin de siècle*. Everybody's depressed."

He ignored the remark as an irrelevance, and as he shifted the angle of his gaze, I could see that he was calculating the precise degree of my probable ignorance.

"Have you ever heard the term 'germ-line cell therapy'?" he asked. "Do you know how many thousands of human embryos are lying around in cold storage?"

I said that I had heard rumors about the human embryos but had assumed that most of them were harmless. The young man regarded me with a superior smile, as if from a cold and condescending height. Identifying himself as a doctoral candidate at the Yale Divinity School, he asked me whether I had noticed either of the two reports published on the front page of the *New York Times* within the space of the last six weeks, one of them about experiments with the sperm cells of mice at the University of Pennsylvania, the other about a mouse inflated with a gene causing it to become grotesquely obese. I remembered the photograph of the fat mouse, which had a bow around its neck and looked to be about the size of a pet rabbit.

"If they can eliminate the gene for obesity," he said, "it's only a matter of time before they can eliminate the gene for sloth."

Before the train reached Bridgeport he had informed me that the news in the biomedical sciences was by no means good. He had been diligently collecting journal articles about transgenic fish and children born to their grandmothers, also newspaper dispatches about the molecular rearrangement of cows and dinosaurs soon to be hatched from old rocks. The new biological world order, he said, was much nearer in time than anybody supposed. Becoming suddenly animated and beginning to wave his hands, he lurched into a projection of the life forms likely to inhabit the next millennium.

"Synthetic salmon as big as killer whales, my friend. Huge and omnivorous creatures devouring all the minor fish in the Gulf of Alaska. Mutant tomatoes as round as basketballs. Insects in the shape of parakeets. Chickens crossed with rats or Quentin Tarantino."

Apparently what troubled him was the prospect of a world from which all traces of human imperfection had been removed, like mud on a boot or stains on a rug. Who then would have need of his services? Of what use was the Old or New Testament among people bred to the design specifications of Steven Spielberg or Donna Karan?

"Perhaps you can explain to me," he said, "the point of preaching sermons to people who look like Yoda and know nothing of sin and remorse."

"Journalists like to write about miracles," I said. "They exaggerate things."

The young man dismissed the objection with an abrupt and impatient gesture, and between Bridgeport and Darien he summed up the result of his research in so rapid a rush of words that I had trouble keeping track of the distinctions between "xenografts" and "the genome project," between the "polymerase chain reaction" and Cenozoic insects preserved in beads of amber. Other passengers came and went, but the divinity student took no notice of them, and he never once was at a loss for another terrible sign or portent looming just below the biomedical horizon. In the station at Stamford he mentioned the 200 genetically engineered organisms released into the environment over the last ten years (all of them suspect and some of them missing), and passing through Cos Cob he mocked the pretensions of literary theorists.

"At Yale," he said, "people think deconstruction is something that happens in the English department." And then, with scornful laughter, "Guys in beards writing commentaries about Proust. They think of themselves as revolutionaries."

But it is the cellular biologists, he said, who revise the texts of human meaning, adding or deleting gene sequences like semicolons. By the time the train entered Westchester County, the divinity student had worked himself into so agitated a state of mind, part despairing prophecy and part antic improvisation, that he had attracted the respectful attention of three teenage girls wearing red woolen caps that made them look like Christmas elves. The apocalyptic tenor of his remarks followed from his assumption that within a matter of not too many years the wonders of corporate science would bring forth a market in genetic home improvements (intelligence, skin color, athletic ability, and so on) as profitable as the market in cosmetics.

"If I can give my dog blue eyes and a dancer's feet," he said, "why can't I do the same for my daughter?"

As long ago as February 1993, he said, the United States government approved the patenting of new life forms, and by so doing granted genetic engineers the right to own specific traits and characteristics. The Patent Office's ruling pertained to animals, but in view of the 1980 Supreme Court decision that the patent laws refer to "anything under the sun made by man," the divinity student foresaw the arrival of the biomedically engineered Eden in three stages, all of them brief.

First, the deployment of the genetic codes to fend off hereditary diseases. Identify the gene for obesity or breast cancer, remove it from the embryo and thus preserve the child from at least one of the scourges of the flesh.

Next and not long afterward, the molecular biologies made to serve the pleasures of the rich. Philip II of Spain collected dwarfs, and what was to prevent the latter-day lords of creation—Michael Jackson, say, or Matsushita, or Bill Gates—from collecting centaurs or two-headed golfers or miniature reproductions of Henry Kissinger? The divinity student could imagine private zoos in Colorado; limited editions issued by the Franklin Mint; bizarre auctions under the chandeliers at Sotheby's.

Last, once the techniques had become both reliable and cheap, the better drug- and department stores selling celebrity-sponsored sperm cells as if they were shades of lipstick. The masculine and feminine ideals of beauty no longer would need to be left to chance, and instead of taking up the questions of faith and conscience, people would graze like sheep among the displays of attractively designed tubes, priced at $49.95 and filled with genetic reprints of Elizabeth Taylor's eyes or Frank Sinatra's voice.

"Who will want to listen to the word of God," he said, "when they can change themselves into whales or movie stars?" The three girls looked at him in amazement, obviously thrilled with the news of their deliverance.

At the station in New Rochelle the train stopped for nearly ten minutes, and the young man fell abruptly silent. His long exigesis apparently had exhausted him without relieving him of his depression. He stared bleakly at the passengers crowding through the doors, most of them noisily excited with the hope of a festive evening in the city, and I wondered what I could say to him that might bring him some small measure of holiday cheer.

He was undoubtedly overstating the speed of scientific advancements (as well as confusing the practice of genetics with the theory of eugenics), but if I was sure that the new biomedical dispensation would arrive at a much later date than he supposed, I was also sure that on his principal existential point his fears were well founded. The pitiless logic of the capital markets eventually would overrule the moral objections from the sentimentalists in the choir loft. The Pope and Pat Buchanan might rail against the blasphemy of commercial mutation, but the bioengineering industries already have invested as much as $30 billion toward the manufacture of improved human beings, and too much money stands to be made from the sale of a heart-shaped mouth or a longer life.

If I couldn't comfort the divinity student with psalms, at least I could console him with assurances about the vanity and greed of his fellow man. I remembered that the Yale Divinity School had been founded in a very strict and Puritan tradition, and the faculty possibly had neglected to introduce the young man to the writings of the more sardonic authors. I suspected that he had read too much of Thomas Aquinas and not enough of Voltaire; too much Martin Buber and John Bunyan, not enough Mark Twain and Ambrose Bierce.

"Have faith in Mammon," I said, "and trust to the quibbling of lawyers. Rely on the cowardice of politicians."

The train slowed down for its passage through the desolation of the South Bronx, and I explained that whereas the devil offered Faust knowledge and power in return for his soul, the modern corporations would offer traits and characteristics for a percentage of the gross and that, with any luck, the lawsuits would last a thousand years.

The trace of an approving smile flickered briefly at the corners of the divinity student's mouth, but then he thought of the numberless charlatans unable to resist the temptation of promising biological utopia, probably not much different in its landscape of good behaviors than the one envisioned by the Republican signers of the Contract with America—Sunday school rows of obedient citizens, all of them blameless and most of them blond, none of them committing crimes, nobody telling lies.

"I can hear the speeches," he said. "No more racial hatred. No more citizens physically or intellectually challenged. An end to war and aggression, and literacy furnished at birth. Welcome to the New Jerusalem."

I assured him that even the Christian Coalition would come to its senses and everyone would remember that the end of war is also the end of finance capitalism, that by relieving the human race of its stupidity and grief, the apostles of everlasting happiness also would be evicting themselves from the office in Washington and the pulpit in Palm Springs.

The young man frowned, still worried about the lack of souls to save, and I again assured him that although nobody could afford to put the proposition quite so plainly, a consensus of the country's best and most respectable opinion would discover that an excess of virtue debases the currency of free will and subverts the meaning of the Constitution. The train was on the railroad bridge crossing the East River into Queens, and out the windows to the west we could see the triumphant Manhattan skyline glittering in the dusk.

"Of what else is the city made," I said, "except the sins of mankind?"

Without avarice, I said, what would become of Wall Street? Deprive a broker of his inalienable right to insider trading, and the market would empty of both buyers and sellers. Without lust, what would happen to the news and entertainment media? The few remaining journalists would be reduced to making lists of yesterday's temperature readings. Without wrath, who would go to see Steven Seagal movies or the Super Bowl? Without pride, what hairdresser could schedule an afternoon's appointments? What tailor could sell another suit? Delete the stain of envy from the national genome, and the entire apparatus of the American economy—the glory of its markets and the grandeur of its laws, the whole magnificent edifice of steel and glass and neon light— would crumble as surely into dust as the colossal wreck of Troy.

"It would never do, you see," I said. "Human perfection is the ruin of the state."

In Pennsylvania Station a Salvation Army band was playing "Joy to the World." The young man walked with me toward Seventh Avenue, both of us pushing against the current of the holiday crowd festooned with shopping bags from Tiffany's and Bloomingdale's and The Gap. But in all that vast throng of wayward souls, hurrying home to Christmas and the suburbs, bearing overpriced gifts and long lists of New Year's promises they already knew they couldn't keep, I noticed very few who didn't look to be angry or tired or late. Reminded of the vanity of human wishes and the heavy burden of human sorrow wrapped up in so many red and green ribbons, I clapped the student on the back and told him to take heart, rejoice in the spirit of the season and know that he saw before him a lifetime guarantee of steady work.

"Fear not," I said. "Even if by some mischance Bristol-Myers Squibb isolates the gene for peace on earth and goodwill toward men, the poor couldn't afford it and the rich would want something more amusing."

The young man almost smiled—not as yet a broad smile, not a smile that anybody would associate with Santa Claus or think to put on a Hallmark Card, but nonetheless a brighter expression than the one with which he had boarded the train in New Haven. In the distance I could hear the Salvation Army trumpet taking up the tune of "Good King Wenceslaus," and as the divinity student walked off into the traffic and the rain changing to snow, I thought I noticed a stronger set to his shoulders, as if somehow it had occurred to him that toy mice and the futures market both bear witness to the art of God.

*February 1995*

# Tower of Babel

The better the technology, the less efficient the human use of it.
—AUGUST FRUGÉ

*F*or the last seven or eight months, I've been listening to people complain about the lack of anything to watch on television, and I notice that as their options multiply—from ten cable channels to thirty, from thirty channels to seventy-five—so also does the degree of their nervousness and discontent. A few days before President Clinton's inauguration, I spoke to a man who had wired what he called his "situation room" with no fewer than one hundred channels, but the wealth of possibility had failed to give him joy, and he was bewildered by the emptiness of the view.

"I don't expect you to believe me," he said, "but at ten o'clock last night, there was nothing on."

He was alarmed as well as confused, and I wondered what would become of him when the cable operators deliver, as they have promised to do over the next two or three years, as many as 750 channels. I could imagine him in a state of near panic, pushing frantically at the buttons of his remote-control device, rushing through the channels in search of he knew not what.

The good old days of the network monopolies begin to look like the good old days of the Cold War. Everybody knew who was who and what was what, and the truths told by Walter Cronkite or Johnny Carson were as certain as the border crossings between the capitalist paradise and the communist inferno. But now that the world has slipped the bonds of military empire, it is besieged by the fevers of nationalism—in what was once Yugoslavia and colonial Africa as well as in what was once the Soviet Union. Transposed into the idiom of American television, the parallel expressions of anarchy and irredentism take the form of Rush Limbaugh or Howard Stern, and the façade of cultural imperialism crumbles into the separatist states of moral feeling elected to office by a hand-held camera, a 900 telephone number and a rented studio on Santa Monica Boulevard. The season's political candidates travel the pilgrim road of the tabloid talk shows, making confession to Larry or Barbara or Phil, and in the distant reaches of the cable system, once-upon-a-time celebrities drift like dead moons. On one channel or another, twenty-four hours a day, if not in New York, then in Los Angeles or Chicago or Miami, Gary Cooper and Clint Eastwood teach antithetical lessons in the theory of American justice.

The networks do what they can to sustain the illusion of a common store of value or a unified field of emotion, but their news programs have begun to look like the dioramas at Gettysburg or Epcot Center. I watch Dan Rather interview President Clinton at the White House, and I think of two actors on loan from the Smithsonian, replicating the language of democratic union for the benefit of an audience steadily diminishing in coherence and size.

The incessant division of the American public into the subsections of special interest (cultural and intellectual as well as racial and commercial) spawns the invention of a thousand jargons in which the parties of like-minded sentiment speak chiefly to themselves—lawyer to lawyer, weapons analyst to weapons analyst, literary critic to literary critic, economist to economist.

Four weeks before the release of last year's movie *Malcolm X*, Spike Lee, the director, said that he would prefer to grant interviews only to journalists who were black. Two years ago in New York, while I was taking part in a public discussion of American policy toward Israel, I was informed by a member of the audience that because I was not a Jew my opinions on the subject were worthless. At several of the nation's leading universities the novels of Jane Austen and George Eliot have been remanded to the department of women's studies, the texts subject to explication only by female professors of literature.

The separate audiences recede from one another literally at the speed of light, and the binding curve of technology (satellite transmissions, simultaneous translations into Spanish or Greek, television sets that can choose their own camera angles, and so on) cannot hold together what Sir Richard Livingstone, a former vice-chancellor of Oxford, once described as a "civilization of means without ends." The poor souls searching desperately through the cable channels find themselves lost in the land of the perpetual present, hounded by the desire to grasp or consume, simultaneously, every scrap of vicarious feeling or experience—the glimpse of the half-naked girl on a beach in Rio de Janeiro, the news of next year's financial calamity as foretold by a politician seen briefly on C-SPAN, the last days of the Third Reich as portrayed in an old newsreel, the dawn rising over the Matterhorn and the sun dropping below the horizon at Java Head. Why compound their anxiety? Why burden them with another 650 proofs of their failure to keep up with the times?

When confronted with this line of objection, the would-be impresarios of channels 101 through 749 speak of the inexhaustible need for information and personal services. I don't envy them the task of filling in the empty space and time, but I have no doubt of their ingenuity, and over the next few years I expect them to astonish the world with the marvels of postmodern aesthetics. The more obvious possibilities consist of repetitions or variations of the current programming—another forty or fifty channels given over to narrowly defined categories of sexual experience, the home shopping networks transformed into illustrated catalogues (for L. L. Bean, Horchow, J. Crew, Bloomingdale's) and maybe a hundred channels following obscure sporting events (badminton tournaments, prep-school soccer)—but even these will not be enough to blot out the horizons of thought, and as further extensions of the present trend I can imagine several lines of likely development:

1. *Medical Cinema Verité.* A variation on the theme of courtroom television. Four cameras in an operating room (one

of them overhead) make a continuous record of the work-in-progress. Two or three retired doctors provide commentary in the manner of the retired athletes doing sports broadcasts. They describe the nature of the operation, remark on the surgeon's technique, guess at the patient's chance of survival.

2. *Elvis.* Hourly reports from people who have just run across him in Paris or El Segundo, California.

3. *Tours of Inspection.* Unedited footage of surveillance cameras posted in banks, office buildings, movie theaters, hotels, parking lots and department stores. The primary audience presumably would consist of conspiracy theorists and latter-day Puritans, the kind of people who believe the nation's property and morals must always be closely watched. The show might attract as a secondary audience the merely curious, gossips hoping to see somebody they know checking into a hotel in Dallas when he or she was supposed to be visiting a relative in St. Louis.

4. *Ramtha and Friends.* Conversations with various spirits, druids, Cro-Magnon men, Egyptian queens, departed saints. Sometimes the guests speak in their own voices and languages, sometimes through their mediums or channels. On gala occasions they speak to one another, but they do so only on days that coincide with a solstice, an equinox, or a lunar eclipse.

5. *Time Past.* Several channels (376 through 382, or 523 through 535) broadcasting from the historical coordinates of a prior century or era. On one channel the year is always 1846 in America, on another it is 1791 in Georgian London or 1938 in Nazi Germany. Everything is of the period—the clothes, the furniture, the food, the topics of conversation. People come and go, talking about public events as well as their own domestic affairs. The plots and subplots matter less than the costumes and the sets.

6. *Clouds.* Continuous weather reports from distant deserts and seas. A correspondent posted at the Strait of Magellan reports on wave heights and wind velocities as well as sightings of obscure birds. The show could serve as the sentence of exile for older personnel whom the networks have declared superfluous: a woman makes a mistake with the news from Washington, and she's next seen in the Falkland Islands; an anchorman forgets to dye his hair and he goes directly to the Sea of Azov.

7. *The Last of Their Kind.* Encounters with endangered species. The host, an eminent naturalist, sits across the table from the Florida black bear or the notorious spotted owl and accepts telephone calls from people who wish to express their opinions of the environment. Sometimes the bear nods or the owl frowns. Most of the guests would be plants.

8. *Me.* The life and times of ordinary individuals presented as works of performance art. Chosen at random, from lists of names or because the producer happened to see the person in an elevator or on the street, the newfound celebrities go about the habitual routine of their daily lives. The camera follows them as they do their laundry or their hair, go to their exercise class, eat breakfast, look into a book or newspaper, swat flies, sharpen a pencil, form an occasional sentence.

Sooner or later the technology will make it possible to divide the American public into audiences of one. The camera shot is that of the distracted viewer in the chair, surrounded by the splendor of consumer electronics and armed with the remote-control device that becomes a queen's scepter or a wand with which wizards summon images from a mirror or a pool of standing water. In the brief instant when the viewer changes one channel for another, obliterating the face of the rival celebrity and replacing it with his own, he can imagine that an audience of one is also the government of Ruritania or the will of God.

*March 1993*

# The Spring Shows

> If it was necessary to tolerate in other people everything that
> one permits in oneself, life would be unbearable.
> —GEORGES COURTELINE

*D*uring the first two weeks in March, five prospective
Republican presidents declared themselves available for
next year's nomination, and the impression was that of
runway models parading across the stage of a fashion show—walk,
flounce, pause, stare (with attitude) at the important buyers of
department-store political product; turn, pout, walk, and wait to
see who sends money. Not surprisingly, none of the candidates—
George W. Bush (governor of Texas), Lamar Alexander (former
governor of Tennessee), Patrick Buchanan (renowned journalist),
Steve Forbes (heir to a swell fortune), and Elizabeth Dole (faithful
wife)—said anything likely to upset the editors of *Women's Wear
Daily* or the *New York Times*. They chose to be seen, not heard;
to exhibit, with dapper gestures and modish styles of rhetorical
address, the sense of moral elegance that had been missing from
the nation's banquet circuit ever since President Bill Clinton (a

vulgar person and a tasteless lout) had moved into the White House with his saxophone and his bongo drum.

Together with an impressive lack of relevant experience, the five candidates brought to the spring shows their belief that under the influence of Clinton's appalling example, the American people had fallen into slovenly sexual habits, forgotten their table manners, lost respect for the rule of law. Such behavior could not be allowed to continue. The time had come for everybody in the social studies class to pay attention and look at the picture of Teddy Roosevelt, and how better to begin than by admiring the manliness of Buchanan, the piety of Alexander, the lineage of Bush, the net worth of Forbes, the gender of Dole?

Admire, not bother with questions. Forbes put up his show on the Internet (complete with a portfolio of designs from his 1996 campaign); Dole declined to speak to reporters when making her announcement to a preferred audience at a convention hall in Des Moines. Introduced by four local citizens pressed into service as allegories (a farmer, a working mother, a high-school teacher, a twelve-year-old girl), the candidate said that she had made herself manifest in human form because she wanted to combat "evil in American society." No, she didn't have any ideas, at least not yet, but very, very soon, after she had listened to the voice in the divine cloud of the opinion polls, she would know what people wanted to hear, and then she would bring them bandages and apple pies. She was no politician ("and frankly, I think that's a plus today") but just a woman, a wonderful, wonderful woman, of course, who had been appointed to all these wonderful, wonderful government offices in Washington and knew a lot of wonderfully important people, not least among them her husband, the once-upon-a-time senator and doomed presidential candidate, his image recently revived by cosmetic surgery and his Q-rating enhanced by his appearances as a television shill for penile resurrection. Maybe in a month or two Mrs. Dole would know what to say about Kosovo or welfare reform, but in the meantime, and while her speechwriters were dealing with the paperwork, here she was, the Queen of Hearts, wearing her wonderful red suit and her wonderful pearls.

In contrast to Mrs. Dole's trunk show, Mr. Bush presented his line of civic-minded sportswear in the manner of a Paris opening. Lots of flashbulbs, the splendor of the Governor's Mansion in Austin, Texas, ten testimonials instead of four, dignified Republican personages seated among the potted ferns, strong endorsements ("the best of the Republican Party," "Lincoln, Reagan—and now, George W. Bush"), an audience buzzing with the presence of New York fund-raising consultants, Hollywood voice coaches, once and future secretaries of state.

The candidate smiled for the cameras, paced back and forth on the dais to show that his tie had lost nothing of its old Episcopalian swing; but no, he didn't wish to say anything other than "It's George W. Bush that's going to be the president; any rival who criticizes my father makes a huge mistake." The bravura of the setting was sufficient to the purpose, and why spoil the effect with impromptu remarks? The brand name spoke for itself; Bush was right there in the stores with Hugo Boss—"vibrant,"

"conservative," "well-connected," "compassionate," in tune with
the trend away from Monica and the Blowfish.

Buchanan announced in New Hampshire, the state in which
he had defeated Mrs. Dole's then-unrejuvenated husband in the
1996 primary campaign; Alexander announced in Nashville, Tennessee, in the state capitol where he once had occupied the office
of governor. Because neither candidate could afford the price of
glamour—no balloons, no band music, no celebrities stopping by
on their way to East Hampton or Brentwood, nothing to show
that hadn't already been seen in Macy's or on *The McLaughlin
Group*—the presentations lacked panache. The poses were out-
dated, the couture a little sad, and most of what was on view was
the vanity of the gentlemen handing out their own press releases.
Buchanan dressed his small and poorly lighted stage in Manchester
with slogans instead of flags, exhorting his sparse audience
(middle-aged and wary, the women wearing windbreakers, the
men wearing boots and winter caps) to protect "the rights of the
innocent unborn," to "call down the curtain on the sorry soap
opera in the White House," to "mount up and ride to the sound
of the guns." Which guns and where pointed Buchanan didn't
say, possibly because he was without a cell phone and not closely
enough in touch with Private Ryan. Nor did he appear to be in
close touch with the shifts in the public mood since his name was
last on the ballot in New Hampshire. Drawing on the furious
vocabulary of late-nineteenth-century populism, he raged against
the selfish greed in Wall Street; the rhetoric was as crude and as
gaudily colored as a poster promoting Buffalo Bill Cody at the
1893 Chicago World's Fair, but it didn't excite the passions of

people comforted by the stock-market prices that in early March were reaching record highs.

Candidate Alexander at least had taken the trouble to read the papers; knowing that his image needed a thorough makeover, he had abandoned his theme as the honest man from nowhere, the outside-of-Washington teller of country truths last seen in a red plaid shirt in the 1996 primary campaign and reported missing somewhere in the mountains west of Chattanooga. No sir, no more Mr. Bluegrass. The governor showed up in a dark suit and red tie—a new persona, an inside-the-Beltway kind of guy, glad to sit in anybody's lobby, proud to say that when he walked into the White House he would know "from the first day . . . exactly what to do." His tone echoed the complacence of Steve Forbes, who had informed his friends on the Internet that whereas President Clinton had given the American people a government to be "ashamed of," President Forbes would give them a government to be "proud of."

Because the five declarations of presidential intent occurred within the short span of fifteen days, they could be seen as segments of the same montage, and the humor of the proceedings followed from the several degrees of separation between the candidates on the runway and the audiences on whom they bestowed the favor of their great good news. The would-be presidents spoke from the rostra of wealth and privilege, if not possessed of their own substantial fortunes then bankrolled by the moneyed interests who could afford to bet $60 million on the roulette table of a presidential campaign. None of them wished to change or remake the world, and nobody, not even Buchanan, was talking about revolution. Why should they? Who in his or her right mind would want to harm the system that provided them with their hairstylists and their microphones?

Absent any threatening political content or purpose, the presentations substituted style for substance, religion for government, questions of personal conduct for those of public policy. The candidates differed on narrow points of doctrine—Buchanan opposed to abortion in any and all circumstances, Dole, Bush, Alexander, and Forbes willing to grant exceptions for rape—but they were unanimous in the opinion that nothing was wrong with American society that couldn't be corrected by prompt improvements in the American character. The country was rich and happy and ripe with golden opportunity, but too many of its citizens had become careless and disruptive (also promiscuous, surly, overweight, and badly dressed); they'd been watching too much bad television, buying too many jellied condoms and anarchic rap songs, lying around too long in the Florida sun. Fortunately all was not lost. The slackers had only to behold the candidates standing before them to know that salvation was near at hand. Behold, admire, learn by example if not by rote. Civility, my friends, decency, ethics, pearls; get hold of yourselves, read the *Wall Street Journal*, and *Martha Stewart Living* and remember that one never wears cashmere in the rain.

\*    \*    \*

The rendering of politics as fashion statement no doubt can be understood as proof of the country's immense prosperity and a tribute to the success of its experiments with virtual reality. A four-year lease on the White House costs a good deal less than a low-wattage radio station in Wichita, Kansas, and why begrudge a red-blooded and well-meaning American plutocrat the pleasure of playing with the Washington toys? It's still early in the season, and we have yet to hear from Rosie O'Donnell or Donald Trump. Let the Dow Jones Industrial Average approach the altitude of 15,000 points and maybe we can change politics into aesthetics and thus discover a candidate as engaging as the Roman emperor Nero, another wealthy and condescending amateur who sought to amaze his audience with the miracle of his presence.

The standard histories dwell on Nero's cruelty and sexual pathology—his murdering of his mother, the prior emperor, three wives, several hundred near or distant relatives; his dressing himself in the skins of wild animals to stimulate his lust. The old books never fail to tell the apocryphal story about his setting fire to the city of Rome, but they seldom mention his career as an artist. Nero fancied himself as a singer, also as a player of the lyre, and prior to competing for a prize, he reminded the other contestants that if they made the mistake of singing too well they could look forward to the additional honor of an early death. His voice, by all accounts, was feeble and usually out of tune, but he was fond of the Greek proverb "Unheard melodies are never sweet," and no matter how often he repeated the remark it never failed to inspire an agreeable murmur of prompt assent. The emperor almost always preferred the role of soloist, but from time to time he agreed to appear in operatic tragedies, taking the part of a god or goddess improved for the occasion with a mask modeled either on his own face or the face of his current mistress.

When Nero took his act on tour (to Corinth or Naples or Alba Longa) he seldom traveled without an escort of 1,000 carriages, the road before him sprinkled with perfume and the bystanders instructed to shower him with songbirds. Nor did he forget to bring the instruments of sustained applause, a troop of 5,000 young men, splendidly dressed, and divided into three claques known as "Bees" (who made a loud humming noise), "Roof Tiles" (who clapped with cupped hands), and "Brick Bats" (who clapped flat-handed).

Sometimes the emperor sang for seven hours, and during his recitals nobody was allowed to leave the theater. Centurions locked the doors and took attendance. Suetonius speaks of "women in the audience giving birth, of men being so bored with the music and the applause that they furtively dropped down from the walls at the rear, or shammed dead and were carried away for burial."

Judging by the broad lack of response to the Republican spring show, most everybody in the audience managed to make it safely over the walls. The five fashion statements clearly were still in need of a little work—more excitement, maybe satin, maybe hats, possibly songbirds or something in platinum lamé. Between now and the important openings next winter in Iowa and New Hampshire the several design studios presumably will be busy with the tissue paper and the safety pins. But in the meantime the runway models will have to depend upon the Roof Tiles, the Brick Bats, and the Bees, their sound amplified and their numbers much increased by the technological genius of the news and entertainment media. Our modern institutional forms of the ancient Roman practice developed in nineteenth-century France. The owners of Paris theaters employed *claqueurs* in place of publicists, photographers, television talk-show hosts, authors of celebrity interviews; being French and therefore fond of bureaucracy, they established formal degrees of hired praise:

*The Chef de Claque*—who received money from the actors and free tickets from the management. He bribed the critics and paid the lower-ranking touts.

*Commissaires*—who memorized the better parts of the play, which they then brought to the attention of the important theatergoers, among whom they were tactfully placed.

*Rieurs*—who laughed, loudly, during comedies.

*Pleureuses*—women who wept, copiously, during melodramas.

*Bisseurs*—who shouted, frantically, for encores.

The swarm of cameras following Monica Lewinsky on her progress through a Washington airport or a New York restaurant wouldn't have surprised the Roman mob familiar with the expensive claques traipsing after the magnificence of the Emperor Nero, their eager and well-fed sycophancy presumably equivalent to the breathless enthusiasms of Barbara Walters. A careful student of the contemporary media no doubt could place our own latter-day *claqueurs* within the proper categories (Cokie Roberts a *commissaire*, Jerry Springer a *bisseur*, etc.), but I expect that most of the nation's leading commentators, in both the print and broadcast press, would find themselves among the *pleureux*. They have been mourning the loss of America's moral treasure ever since President Clinton's first term in office, and what they perceived as the disappointing result of last winter's impeachment trial prompted copious weeping about the debased character of the American electorate.

Let us hope that the new presidential-campaigning season presents them with reasons to make a joyful humming noise. The Bees enjoy giving of their best (pollinating the orchards of celebrity, supplying the buzz to *Variety* and *Newsweek*), but they like bright colors and the scent of scandalmongered sheets, and unless the politicians attract their fancy—maybe chiffon, maybe sunglasses—they might perish in the autumn frost, and then who will go to the election or dance at the Inaugural Ball?

*May 1999*

# Sky Writing

The moment Kafka attracts more attention than Joseph K.,
Kafka's posthumous death begins.
—MILAN KUNDERA

*O*ne of these days I expect to see the author of a new book
parachute into New York harbor trailing clouds of blue
smoke and playing "Summertime" on the harmonica. If
the book promises big and best-selling news—of war or peace or
the death of conscience—I can imagine the author coming ashore
at Battery Park, resplendent in military uniform and welcomed
by Lee Iacocca and a line of cabaret dancers.

It's no easy trick to drum up interest in something so easily
misplaced as a book, and the writers who still nurture the hope
of readers have been known to try almost anything to attract the
attention of a camera. In a newspaper last week I noticed that a
consultant charges authors $500 an hour for lessons in the tech-
niques of self-promotion. Even if an author can write as well as
Herman Melville or Edith Wharton, literary talent counts for
nothing unless he or she also knows how to sell the book on radio

and television. Some of the less delicate publishing houses now ask to see not only a manuscript but also a videotape of the author telling jokes and cautionary tales.

Under the rules of contemporary society, nobody, not even God, can afford to offend the media. It is all very well to be rich or talented or beautiful or brave, but unless one is known to be rich or talented or beautiful or brave, one cannot be a celebrity, and if one isn't a celebrity, one might as well be dead.

The nobility in seventeenth-century France felt the same way about the brilliantly lit society at Versailles. No matter how magnificent their country estates or how numerous their horses and servants, they believed themselves invisible unless they could make a show at court. But before they could appear at court, they had to know how to walk and curtsy and speak an artificial language that would fall pleasingly on the ear of a duke.

In our own society—a society increasingly obsessed with the flutter of images—the ladies and gentlemen of the media serve as courtiers in the king's palace. Unless one knows how to conduct oneself in their august presence, even the richest of businessmen or the wisest of authors must vanish into the pits of anonymity and ridicule.

Two years ago, by virtue of a coincidence as implausible as it was unexpected, I found myself at what is known as a "media training session" for the chairman of a very large and very greedy insurance company. The gentleman had been invited to an interview on network television, and he was worried about the presentation of his image.

He had reason to be anxious. Insurance companies of late haven't been receiving the best of press notices, and for the modest sum of $10,000 the company in question had hired public relations counsel to give the chairman a one-day lesson in studio etiquette. He arrived promptly at 9 A.M., uneasy and nondescript despite the expensive tailoring of what was obviously a new suit. He was accompanied by seven assistants—the vice president in charge of political affairs, two secretaries, a speechwriter, a statistician, a consultant, and a valet. About the same number of people represented the public relations firm.

Everybody shook hands with everybody else, and the company arranged itself around a long and highly polished table. Somebody named Bernie came briskly to the business at hand. He introduced a troupe of "communications specialists" who would play the part of the television journalists, and then, speaking to the chairman, he said, "What you have to bear in mind is the simplicity of the medium and the stupidity of the hosts. Never answer their questions. Never be seen to think."

The chairman nodded complacently, delighted to hear Bernie confirm his dearest prejudices. Bernie made a few more observations—about dictating the terms of the interview and keeping one's fingers out of one's nose—and everybody moved into an adjoining studio for the first performance. The chairman settled himself into a chair opposite the surrogate host, an aggressively affable young man named Mort, and waited confidently for the first question.

His self-assurance didn't last thirty seconds. Mort smiled a greasy smile and said, "Perhaps you can tell us, Mr. Chairman, why your company gouges people with the viciousness of a Mafia loan shark?"

The chairman's mouth opened and closed like the mouth of a netted fish. Mort accepted his silence as a concession of guilt and went unctuously on to the next question: "I can't say I blame you, Mr. Chairman, but maybe you can tell us why your company robbed its own stockholders of $500 million last month to prevent the merger with E. F. Hutton?"

By an obviously heroic effort, as if struggling with giant snakes, the chairman achieved the victory of speech. It wasn't coherent speech, of course, and none of it resembled the notes on the index cards in the chairman's coat pocket—wonderfully succinct little statements about his company's benevolent service to the American people. Gasping with rage, he managed to say—not very distinctly, but distinctly enough to be heard by 25 million people in the viewing audience—"You're a dirty, lying son of a bitch."

Bernie stopped the camera. In a voice almost as breezy as Mort's, he said, "Yes, well, I can see we have a lot of work to do."

The rest of the day wasn't easy. Mort was sent away, replaced by a woman who wasn't quite so rude. The valet trimmed the chairman's hair; the speechwriter typed the prepared statement in capital letters; the secretary reminded the chairman that he was one of the richest men in the world.

By five that afternoon, the chairman was capable of getting through five minutes in front of the camera without committing a theatrical equivalent of suicide. His retainers helped him out the door, mopping his forehead, steadying his shoulders, murmuring reassurance in his ears. Watching him depart, Mort said: "Believe it or not, he was better than most."

And then, after the door had closed: "It's a wonderful world. Fifty years ago I could have been teaching debutantes to dance."

I assume that the consultant to the literary notables offers more or less the same instruction—maxims about the simplicity of the medium and the need for short sentences, tips and hints about the pitch of one's voice, the color of one's dress, the reduction of a thought to its least common denominator.

Reading the newspaper report of the season's newest authors smiling anxiously into their hired cameras, I thought, sadly, of circus dogs dressed up in funny little costumes, rolling through barrels and balancing clocks on their heads. Something of the same melancholy feeling overcomes me when I see a decent writer talking to Johnny Carson.

Not that writers have much choice in the matter, at least not in America. The native audience for literature never has been large or easily found, and apparently it was never enough for a writer simply to write. The public has always preferred sensations, and it tolerates authors only if they can be seen as freaks and wonders—the sort of people who make scenes in restaurants, supply the newspapers with salacious gossip, discover miraculous cures and new religions.

The work of self-dramatization is as much a proof of the writer's art as the composition of dialogue and the invention of plot. Even in the best of times the successful American writers have adopted the gaudy disguises that admit them to the stage of the national music hall. Walt Whitman and Ezra Pound appeared as mad prophets, Henry James as the aesthete in exile, Mark Twain as a clown, Ralph Waldo Emerson and Jonathan Schell as preachers, Tom Wolfe as a dandy, Norman Mailer as a Caliban or *enfant terrible* who periodically revises the hideousness of his mask to reflect the conventional fear and trembling of the prosperous middle class. In the early 1960s, soon after stabbing his second wife, Mailer wrote, "If you can use a knife, there is still some love left." Twenty years later Mailer sponsored the literary career of Jack Henry Abbott, a self-confessed murderer and psychopath. The boredom of his audience required more violent stimuli, and when Abbott killed a waiter a few days after the publication of his jailhouse memoir, *In the Belly of the Beast*, Mailer told a press conference, "Culture is worth a little risk."

Confronted with the literary success bestowed on the memoirs of wealthy real estate operators and notorious madams, the author who would be king stages his most elaborate productions in the theaters of the self. It is the life, not the book, that becomes the object of art. The choice works against the writing of literature, but not many American writers have the patience or the fortitude to stay out of the publicity mills.

Foreign writers—perhaps because they can rely on the presence of an interested and educated audience—find it easier to accept the blessing of obscurity. I think of John le Carré and Milan Kundera, both of whom define the press interview as a synonym for a hanging. But with few exceptions (among them J. D. Salinger, Thomas Pynchon, and Evan Connell) the American writer is drawn, mothlike, into the klieg light. It is impossible not to admire his recklessness, no matter how far-fetched his prose or how grotesque his gestures and costumes.

To appreciate the achievement of American writers it is necessary to bear in mind the odds against their enterprise. The republic of American letters is invariably in a state of anarchy. Without a canon of common texts or cultural references, without standards, lacking even one critic whose judgment pretends to the weight of authority, barely literate and always receptive to a bribe, the administration of the nation's literary affairs falls naturally into the hands of touts and thieves. The American public doesn't look to the arts—whether painting or drama or literature—for answers to questions that it considers important. It is an opening night crowd, astonished by celebrity and opulent spectacle, willing to applaud whatever the merchants in New York and Los Angeles distribute under the labels of culture.

The writer is always playing against the house, and it's no wonder that he acquires the habits of mind congenial to the political left. It isn't that most American writers care for socialism or believe in the theories of a Utopian future. As often as not they despise socialists and prefer the dream of the Arcadian past.

What aligns them with the predicament of the left is the sense of operating behind enemy lines. Books have so little to do with the business of America that the author imagines himself traveling on a forged passport in a foreign country. He trades in metaphors, but everywhere he goes he discovers people who would rather deal in monuments, who delight not in the play of thought but in the displays of power. The vivid lights of the cities, the Babylonian architecture of the gilded office towers, the rain forests planted in the atria of the chrome-plated hotels—all proclaim the energetic faith of a people in thrall to the miracles of commerce.

Even if he has been outfitted with a trick smile and a new hat, the author cannot help defining himself as a guerrilla in the mountain wilderness of a lost cause, a romantic figure plotting sudden descents on the prosperous sensibility of the seacoast resorts. Possibly this is why so many American writers have distinguished themselves in the shorter forms of literary expression—I think of Bierce's aphorisms, Hemingway's short stories, Vidal's essays, Updike's paragraphs, Mailer's polemics, Plimpton's sketches, Bellow's sermons, Didion's metaphors, Styron's sentences, Heller's one-line jokes. Not that these writers haven't succeeded in the longer forms of the history, the novel, and the tract, but they achieve their most memorable effects under the cover of brevity. Instead of staging long sieges, they conduct brilliant raids. Sometimes the raids entail a criminal arrest or an appearance on the Donahue show; sometimes, on more fanciful or clandestine occasions, a parachute and a plume of blue smoke.

*May 1986*

# *Jefferson on Toast*

Westforth Communications
1340 Avenue of the Americas
New York, New York 10019

April 20, 1995

Harold Goldenson
Aurora Pictures
1805 Avenue of the Stars
Century City, California 90067

Dear Harry,

Between acts of the Stoppard play at Lincoln Center on Tuesday night, Susan Stanton said that she had seen you at the Academy Awards and that you wanted to make a movie that said something important about America. "Harry is really serious about this thing," she said. "He wants something big for a summer release, something in time for the elections." She said you were worried about what's gone wrong with the country.

That's a beautiful thought, Harry, and I know you mean it.
Except for Spielberg, I can't think of any other producer in the
business that has your kind of courage. But Spielberg is a Dem-
ocrat and a friend of Barbra Streisand's, and it's easy to make
movies from the sentimental left. All anybody needs is a conspiracy theory, an endangered species, and a crooked politician who
looks like Michael Caine. You know as well as I, Harry, that it's
always been harder for those of us on the right, particularly in
Hollywood. But if the news from Washington is even close to the
truth, maybe the times have changed and Natalie won't have to
go to Paris to wear her furs.

We've known each other for a lot of years, Harry, and as I've
told you before (both as a friend and as a screenwriter), you're
going to have to start thinking about history. I know you don't
like the idea, and more than once I've heard you say that the kids
these days don't know the difference between Adolf Hitler and
Abraham Lincoln, and that without the kids we've got nothing
at the box office. Nada. No points. No distribution deal. No home
video. Zip. But there's some great stuff in the old books, and you
see what's been playing on the suburban screens—*Rob Roy, The
Madness of King George, The Last of the Mohicans, Jefferson in Paris*.
Maybe the kids can't spell, but they like the clothes.

I also don't know how else you can get across what I think
you're trying to say about where and how the country lost its
moral sense. I've heard you talk about the lack of respect for authority, about the imbecile news media and corporate lawyers who
look and sound like Kato Kaelin. All good points, Harry, and
well worth repeating as often as possible to anybody at the bar at

Spago who has the wit to listen, but I think you make Gingrich's mistake about the Sixties. It wasn't the Sixties that wrecked the place. Things went wrong a long time before the Beatles showed up in the Hollywood Bowl and Charles Manson broke into the house in Benedict Canyon.

As I've also told you more than once, the trouble started with the American Revolution. The wrong side won the war, Harry, and it's about time that somebody said so. For 200 years the British have been taking a very bad rap. They weren't the villains of the piece. Not by any means. You've stayed at Clivedon—two years ago if I remember correctly, during the matches at Wimbledon—and you once had dinner with Larry Olivier. You've met Prince Philip, and so you know what kind of people wrote the Magna Carta and invented constitutional government. People who believed in family values and understood the importance of property. Hearts of oak, Harry, marooned in a godforsaken wilderness in 1765, badgered by ungrateful tinsmiths, fighting for the cause of Western civilization.

If you saw *The Madness of King George*, you'll remember the last scene, when the king has recovered his wits and stands with his wife and sons on the steps of a palace, acknowledging the cheers of his loyal subjects. "Smile at the people," he says to the Queen and the Prince of Wales. "Wave to them, let them see that we're here." That's why you want to make the movie, Harry, to impart to our own Anglo-Saxon establishment a similar sense of well-being—to recover for the members of the Los Angeles Country Club the lost belief in their own legitimate authority, to teach somebody else besides Michael Jordan how to smile and wave.

I haven't worked out a script, but at this point I'd urge you to think about the purpose of the film and the sensation that it would be bound to make. Why let Oliver Stone take up all the space on the Op-Ed page of the *New York Times?* With the larger points in mind, I've taken the liberty of making a few notes:

### 1. THE EIGHTEENTH CENTURY

Fairfield County's dream of heaven. Where we would all hope to go if we knew the right travel agent. Look at *Jefferson in Paris* and what do you see? Handsome lawns, lovely buildings, footmen standing behind every chair. The Republican Party in silk. The picture of a world that doesn't worry itself about class privilege and the distance between the rich and the poor. Carriages drive through the rabble in the streets of Paris in 1776, and the ladies and gentlemen on their way to a costume ball or a fireworks display don't feel obliged to wonder whether the horses might be trampling to death an occasional orphan. Even more to the point, it's easy to tell the difference between the superior and inferior classes. The former wear ruffles and brocade and amuse themselves with gossip about the political and sexual scandals of the day. The latter appear in rags, filthy and gap-toothed, shaking their fists and shouting unintelligible obscenities.

The audience experiences a feeling of relief. If so noble an age as that of the eighteenth-century Enlightenment could tolerate without guilt or remorse so lopsided a division of the world's wealth, then why should those of us here in a theater in Westwood fret about the new economic order emerging from the financial chaos of the late twentieth century?

As long ago as 1981 I remember you saying that democracy was an idea whose time had come and gone. You were on your way to Washington for Reagan's inauguration, and we were talking book deals at the Regency Hotel with a New York literary agent who thought that Jimmy Carter was a friend of the common man. "Some of us were born to pick ties on Rodeo Drive," you said then, "and others of us were born to pick lettuce in Salinas." A wonderful line, Harry, and, as always, you were ahead of the polls—ahead of Bill Casey, ahead of Buchanan and Limbaugh, even ahead of Henry Kravis and Martha Stewart.

Think of the *ancien régime* as an advertisement for the great, good American place—like an expensive Virginia suburb, or a well-run golf resort in Scottsdale, Arizona—and you have the beginning of a movie about what was lost to the world at Saratoga in the autumn of 1777. Believe me, Harry, you'll be doing your countrymen a favor. They're rich, but they don't know how to behave. Merchant Ivory have made their production company into a school of manners, and Scorsese attempted the trick in *The Age of Innocence*, but nobody has your brio, Harry, and nobody else can teach Cleveland how to walk on parquet.

## 2. THE AMERICAN REBELS

Most of them were debtors and tax cheats, and when they weren't smuggling contraband (usually rum but sometimes tea or slaves), they were forever dividing into quarrelsome factions, imagining rights where none existed and complaining about affronts to their dignity. Britain financed the Seven Years' War against the Indians and the French, paying for the defense of New

England and granting God knows how much government money to people who thought that Parliament owed them a comfortable living. And what was the response when the crown attempted to reduce the subsidy? Insolence and rebellion. Speeches in Boston's Faneuil Hall as wrongheaded as the editorials in the *New York Times* complaining about the taking away of the welfare soup. Sam Adams was as much of a malcontent as Anthony Lewis or Mary McGrory, as far off the wall as Noam Chomsky, and as badly dressed as William Kunstler.

We would need to be careful with the major figures. If seen at all, they should be seen in passing or in the distance, their wigs slightly askew and their characters just enough at odds with the standard portraits to cast doubt on their objections to the British monarchy. We see in Washington his love of uniforms and portentous silences, a man forever posing for a marble statue; Jefferson talks too much and James Otis drinks; in Lafayette we see the self-importance of somebody like Donald Trump; and in Tom Paine, a stubborn intransigence that finally buried him in a pauper's grave.

The loyal American Tories occupy the foreground of the story, sober and well-to-do merchants who sent to London for their gold-headed canes and to Paris for their wine. People who kept faith with the crown of England—i.e., the original Contract with America. All men of property and sense, Harry, like most everybody you know in Bel-Air, people who saw, all too clearly, what was likely to become of a country given over to the passions of the mob and the theories of Jean-Jacques Rousseau.

Susan said that you wanted a piece of paper before the end of the week, but my notes are in the house at East Hampton, and my memory doesn't serve me as well as it once did. The names of a number of worthy characters nonetheless come more or less readily to mind: Thomas Hutchinson in Boston, who wept on reading the account of Charles I's beheading; Mather Byles, who asked, correctly as it turns out, "Which is better—to be ruled by one tyrant three thousand miles away or by three thousand tyrants not one mile away?"; the Reverend James Maury, of Fredericksburg, Virginia, a principled clergyman and no stranger to the canon of great books, who put his classical education to practical use in the naming of his slaves—Clio, Cato, Ajax, and Cicero.

Hutchinson was the lieutenant governor of the Massachusetts Colony in the 1760s and by all reports a decent and honorable man. During the Stamp Act Riots the Boston mob tore down his house, literally board by board, smashing the windows, splintering the furniture, dragging the contents of the house (plates, books, portraits, children's clothes) into the muddy street. He was a justice of one of the Crown courts, and the next morning he appeared on the bench in borrowed clothes, and with tears in his eyes he made what even the most zealous patriots present recognized as a particularly fine and affecting speech.

Susan also said that you were anxious to find a role for Uma Thurman, so you should look up the life of Elizabeth Loring, who was known to the Boston newspapers in the 1770s as "a brilliant and unprincipled woman," "the flashing blonde," or, more simply, "the Sultana." Shortly after the Battle of Bunker Hill she seduced Sir William Howe, the general in command of the British army, who found her so engaging that he delayed by six months his assault on Philadelphia. By way of a courtesy to the lady's husband, Howe appointed him a commissary of army prisons in Boston. Loring returned the favor by starving to death most of the American prisoners in his care.

If you choose to make the movie, you almost certainly would want to exploit the character of Gouverneur Morris, a New York aristocrat who wrote the Constitution but retained a profound contempt for democratic theory. He later served as the American ambassador in Paris, and remained in that city (the only foreign representative to do so) during the Reign of Terror. A man of courage, intelligence, and resource, Harry, who shared with Talleyrand the affections of the Comtesse de Flahaut (another possibility for Thurman, or maybe Heather Locklear). When Morris was set upon one afternoon in the Rue de Rivoli by an angry mob intent on hanging him from the nearest tree as an Englishman and a spy, he unfastened his wooden leg, waved it above his head, and proclaimed himself an American who had lost a limb fighting for liberty. The speech was as false as the leg. Morris had suffered his misfortune while escaping through a window from the husband of one of his mistresses—an accident the standard texts still attribute to an overturned carriage or a drunken coachman—but the Paris crowd, as poorly informed and as easily gulled as Costner, congratulated him with a round of spontaneous applause.

As I say, I don't have my notes at hand, but if you decide to go forward with the project, it won't be hard to hire sympathetic historians capable of filling in the architecture and the hats.

### 3. THE PRODUCTION

Exquisitely photographed, at least three hours long, and with a lot of philosophical speeches about how the dream of liberty and equality always ends up with Robespierre and the guillotine or with Napoleon in the Russian snow. You saw the reviews of *Jefferson in Paris*, and I'm sure you noticed the adjectives—"Opulent," "Lavish," "Elegant," "Gorgeously costumed," "First-class." The critics might as well have been describing a Caribbean beach hotel or the menu at Le Cirque. They loved it, Harry, because they had come to see what civilization was supposed to look like. Footmen running with torches in front of the carriages! Gold lace! Montgolfier's balloon in the garden at Versailles! Wigs! People speaking French! My God, Harry, the Enlightenment!

Believe me when I tell you that you can't miss with this idea. The Republican Party over the last ten years (courtesy of its television and radio and multimedia shows) has prepared the modern audience for the happy return to what the American Tories called "Loyalty and Royalty." I don't know who you get to write or direct, but the casting should be as straightforward as possible: the pretty people (Daniel Day-Lewis, Demi Moore, Redford) as the British aristocracy and the character actors (Randy Quaid, Tommy Lee Jones, Sigourney Weaver, Tarantino) playing the parts of the colonists. In London we see beautiful women posing for Romney and naval officers brilliantly arrived from Lord Nelson's Mediterranean squadron. Philadelphia looks as poor as threadbare Zagreb or Port-au-Prince. You also might want to consider cameo appearances by the leading figures of the age—Mozart at Kew,

Casanova talking about the rustic charms of American women, Talleyrand and Benedict Arnold meeting in the inn at Falmouth.

Susan said that if Pete Wilson becomes president you probably will become the next director of the Voice of America. Make this movie the way I know you can, Harry, and you're more likely to become our ambassador to the Court of St. James's.

When I showed these notes to Susan, she was so excited that she wanted to send somebody to Palio for champagne. "Only Harry," she said. "Only Harry has got the courage to do this thing." She thought that you probably could get Edgar Bronfman to put up the studio money if you convinced him that the movie would win a prize at Cannes.

I'm in the country over the weekend. Let me know when you're ready to talk.

As ever,
David

*June 1995*

# A Man and His Pig

*T*oward the end of last month I received an urgent telephone call from a correspondent on the frontiers of the
higher technology who said that I had better begin
thinking about pigs. Soon, he said, it would be possible to grow
a pig replicating the DNA of anybody rich enough to order such
a pig, and once the technique was safely in place, I could forget
most of what I had learned about the consolations of literature
and philosophy. He didn't yet have the details of all the relevant
genetic engineering, and he didn't expect custom-tailored pigs to
appear in time for the Neiman-Marcus Christmas catalogue, but
the new day was dawning a lot sooner than most people supposed,
and he wanted to be sure that I was conversant with the latest
trends.

At first I didn't appreciate the significance of the news, and I
said something polite about the wonders that never cease. With
the air of impatience characteristic of him when speaking to the
literary sector, my correspondent explained that very private pigs
would serve as banks, or stores, for organ transplants. If the owner
of a pig had a sudden need for a heart or a kidney, he wouldn't
have to buy the item on the spot market. Nor would he have to

worry about the availability, location, species, or racial composition of a prospective donor. He merely would bring his own pig
to the hospital, and the surgeons would perform the meta-
morphosis.

"Think of pigs as wine cellars," the correspondent said, "and
maybe you will understand their place in the new scheme of
things."

He was in a hurry, and he hung up before I had the chance to
ask further questions, but after brooding on the matter for some
hours I thought that I could grasp at least a few of the preliminary
implications. Certainly the manufacture of handmade pigs was
consistent with the spirit of an age devoted to the beauty of
money. For the kind of people who already own most everything
worth owning—for President Reagan's friends in Beverly Hills
and the newly minted plutocracy that glitters in the show windows of the national media—what toy or bauble could match the
priceless *objet d'art* of a surrogate self?

My correspondent didn't mention a probable price for a pig
made in one's own image, but I'm sure that it wouldn't come
cheap. The possession of such a pig obviously would become a
status symbol of the first rank, and I expect that the animals sold
to the carriage trade would cost at least as much as a Rolls-Royce
or beachfront property in Malibu. Anybody wishing to present an
affluent countenance to the world would be obliged to buy a pig
for every member of the household—for the servants and secretaries as well as for the children. Some people would keep a pig
at both their town and country residences, and celebrities as precious as Joan Collins or as nervous as General Alexander Haig

might keep herds of twenty to thirty pigs. The larger corporations might offer custom-made pigs—together with the limousines, the stock options, and the club memberships—as another perquisite to secure the loyalty of the executive classes.

Contrary to the common belief, pigs are remarkably clean and orderly animals. They could be trained to behave graciously in the nation's better restaurants, thus accustoming themselves to a taste not only for truffles but also for Dom Pérignon and béchamel sauce. If a man needs a new stomach in a hurry, it's helpful if the stomach in transit already knows what's what.

Within a matter of a very few months (i.e., once people began to acquire more respectful attitudes toward pigs), I assume that designers like Galanos and Giorgio Armani would introduce lines of porcine couture. On the East Side of Manhattan, as well as in the finer suburbs, I can imagine gentleman farmers opening schools for pigs. Not a rigorous curriculum, of course, nothing as elaborate as the dressage taught to thoroughbred horses, but a few airs and graces, some tips on good grooming, and a few phrases of rudimentary French.

As pigs became more familiar as companions to the rich and famous, they might begin to attend charity balls and theater benefits. I can envision collections of well-known people posing with their pigs for photographs in the fashion magazines—Katharine Graham and her pig at Nantucket, Donald Trump and his pig at Palm Beach, Norman Mailer and his pig pondering a metaphor in the writer's study.

Celebrities too busy to attend all the occasions to which they're invited might choose to send their pigs. The substitution could not be construed as an insult, because the pigs—being extraordinarily expensive and well dressed—could be seen as ornamental figures of a stature (and sometimes subtlety of mind) equivalent to that of their patrons. Senators could send their pigs to routine committee meetings, and President Reagan might send one or more of his pigs to state funerals in lieu of Vice President Bush.

People constantly worrying about medical emergencies probably wouldn't want to leave home without their pigs. Individuals suffering only mild degrees of stress might get in the habit of leading their pigs around on leashes, as if they were poodles or Yorkshire terriers. People displaying advanced symptoms of anxiety might choose to sit for hours on a sofa or a park bench, clutching their pigs as if they were the best of all possible teddy bears, content to look upon the world with the beatific smile of people who know they have been saved.

I'm sure the airlines would allow first-class passengers to travel to Europe or California in the company of their pigs, and I like to imagine the sight of the pairs of differently shaped heads when seen from the rear of the cabin.

For people living in Dallas or Los Angeles, it probably wouldn't be too hard to make space for a pig in a backyard or garage; in Long Island and Connecticut, the gentry presumably would keep herds of pigs on their estates, and this would tend to sponsor the revival of the picturesque forms of environmentalism favored by Marie Antoinette and the Sierra Club. The nation's leading architects, among them Philip Johnson and I. M. Pei, could be commissioned to design fanciful pigpens distinguished by postmodern allusions to nineteenth-century barnyards.

But in New York, the keeping of swine would be a more difficult business, and so I expect that the owners of expensive apartments would pay a good deal more attention to the hiring of a swineherd than to the hiring of a doorman or managing agent. Pens could be constructed in the basement, but somebody would have to see to it that the pigs were comfortable, well fed, and safe from disease. The jewelers in town could be relied upon to devise name tags, in gold or lapis lazuli, that would prevent the appalling possibility of mistaken identity. If a resident grandee had to be rushed to the hospital in the middle of the night, and if it so happened that the heart of one of Dan Rather's pigs was placed in the body of Howard Cosell, I'm afraid that even Raoul Felder would be hard pressed to work out an equitable settlement.

With regard to the negative effects of the new technology, I could think of relatively few obvious losses. The dealers in bacon and pork sausage might suffer a decline in sales, and footballs would have to be made of something other than pigskin. The technology couldn't be exported to Muslim countries, and certain unscrupulous butchers trading in specialty meats might have to be restrained from buying up the herds originally collected by celebrities recently deceased. Without strict dietary laws I can imagine the impresarios of a *nouvelle cuisine* charging $2,000 for *choucroute de Barbara Walters* or potted McEnroe.

But mostly I could think only of the benign genius of modern science. Traffic in the cities could be expected to move more gently (in deference to the number of pigs roaming the streets for their afternoon stroll), and I assume that the municipal authorities would provide large meadows for people wishing to romp and play with their pigs.

Best of all, terrorists might learn to seize important pigs as proxy hostages. A crowd of affluent pigs would be a lot easier to manage than the passengers on a cruise ship. If the demands for ransom weren't promptly met, the terrorists could roast the imperialist swine and know that they had eaten the marrow of their enemies and sucked the bones of fortune.

*June 1986*

# *Italian Opera*

## Il Grandioso
### *The Cast*

Orlando Grandioso, *slayer of*
*shibboleths* ........Newt Gingrich

Malocchio, *an evil prince* ........Bill Clinton

Gwendolyn the Good ........Peggy Noonan

Beadle, *a sage* ........Alvin Toffler

Der Meisterschelter ........Kenneth Starr

Moth, *a journalist* ........Peter Jennings

Cobweb ........Susan Molinari

Seraphina ........Arianna Huffington

The Duke of Revlon, *a Moor* ........Vernon Jordan

Balthazar ........Robert Bork

Rubato, *a minstrel* ........Rush Limbaugh

Ringwort ........Henry Hyde

Bearpaw ........Dick Armey

### SCENE 1
*—Stormy night in a forest on*
*Kennesaw Mountain*

A band of fierce partisans assembles around a fierce campfire, swearing patriotic oaths, despising platitudes. It is clear they have come in haste. Trouble broods upon the land. An evil prince rules in Washington. The partisans brandish a motley assortment of weapons—shotguns, scythes, Ronald Reagan's magic zither—and they wear a motley assortment of costumes—gypsy shirts, cavalry boots, Viking helmets, a few fishing and duck-shooting hats.

For twenty minutes the partisans sing of their grievances, the bass voices accompanied by a scherzo rhythm in the strings, and through the agitated counterpoint we hear enough of the words (*"cultura brutta," "omosessuale," "madre non sposata"*) to know that the prince is a foul liberal. Rubato emerges from the forest with a dead television anchorperson stretched across his shoulders. He pitches the body into the fire. The excitement in the woodwinds mounts to a triumphant braying of the horns.

The partisans separate, and suddenly in their midst we see, alone in a magenta spotlight, Il Grandioso, slayer of shibboleths, revealer of wisdom. A surprisingly boyish figure, his head cocked to one side like a remarkably alert parrot, Grandioso wears lederhosen and a military cape inherited from an ancestor who died in the Napoleonic Wars. In his left hand he holds the "Contract with America," and with his right hand he sweeps the ostrich plume off his head and sings, in English and a high tenor voice, the stirring march "I Am the Duke of Wellington." The partisans vow to conquer the wicked cities of death and time. They sing *"Dov'è Andata la Libertà?"* and the scene ends with the ensemble rushing resolutely offstage to the sound of kettle drums.

SCENE 2

*—The Rotunda of the Capitol,*
*early afternoon*

The partisans have won through to victory, capturing all the radio stations south of Boston, and the best people in Washington nervously await the coming of their new speaker of eternal truth. Noble lords, gracious ladies, regal lobbyists, miscellaneous oracles, jesters, professors of economics. The orchestra plays waltz music while perfumed servants pour glasses of champagne for the perfumed guests, who respond with hearty gusts of stage laughter. The corps de ballet dances *tableaux vivants* depicting famous scenes in American history—Washington crossing the Delaware, William Jennings Bryan crucified on the cross of gold. Rubato and Cobweb sing the romantic duet "I Never Thought I'd See This Day."

Grandioso enters with an escort of his rough-hewn partisans, who glare suspiciously at the champagne and Cokie Roberts. Bearpaw stabs a well-wisher whom he mistakes for Dan Rather. The orchestra expresses the confusion of sensibilities by giving to the flutes the angry leitmotifs of the forest horns, and after a sustained tremolo in the violins, Gwendolyn the Good restores the sense of general rejoicing with the immortal aria "Bliss to Be Alive." Children distribute flowers. Moth proposes a toast and bravely smashes his glass against the bust of Millard Fillmore. A contented Grandioso, still in lederhosen but now wearing Teddy Roosevelt's campaign hat instead of the ostrich plume, strides downstage center to lead the company in the singing of *"La Via Mia,"* the deathless ode to free enterprise.

## SCENE 3
*—Early morning in an American*
*Opportunities workshop*

Grandioso sits on a high chair in front of a computer monitor, busily revising the history of Western civilization, adding and deleting paragraphs, revoking the sexual license of the 1960s, scattering papers on a stage already littered with blueprints, memoranda, old books. The orchestra seethes and chatters with furious energy. Aides rush in and out with bulletins—from Rupert Murdoch, who wishes to present a gift of money; from Mongolia, where Grandioso has been named the last of the Ming emperors; from Arkansas, where Ringwort and Bearpaw have learned the Spanish word for penis. The Heritage Foundation sends four birdcages the size of newspaper kiosks, in each one of which a tame policy intellectual swings back and forth on its perch, humming 1950s Broadway show tunes. The corps de ballet performs the dance of the Delphic oracles ("The Six Major Changes," "The Five Basic Principles," "The Three Essential Reasons"), which illustrates Grandioso's theory of the universe.

Beadle enters with his pet owl, Grandioso climbs down from

his high chair, and together they declaim the recitativo "The Ideas Are Too Big, the Issues Too Important."

### INTERLUDE FOR THE CORPS DE BALLET

The dancers enact Grandioso's fateful struggle for an important seat aboard Air Force One. Grandioso arrives by limousine at Andrews Air Force Base; Grandioso walks to the plane; Grandioso starts to ascend the stairs.

But no. It's not to be. Grandioso doesn't know how to play hearts, and so he can't sit up front with Malocchio and Moth and the macadamia nuts. An aide-de-camp points imperiously to the ramp at the rear of the plane.

Shock. Horror. Wild alarm. The percussion erupts into a frenzy of chromatic scales. America is no longer a democracy. All men are not created equal.

Grandioso protests, shakes his fists, draws his dagger, lunges at a flight attendant. The dancers rush frantically around the stage, miming the gestures of truth denied, virtue rebuffed. All to no avail. Men in uniform restrain Grandioso and lead him up the ramp with the lettuce and the towels. The music droops into a sullen muttering of oboes. The dancers crumple and fall like wilting flowers.

## SCENE 4
### —The Tidal Basin, dawn

Grandioso gazes pensively into the mist. He now knows that Malocchio is more dreadful than he had thought. More dreadful and far more devious. The music recalls the heroic march from Scene 1 ("I Am the Duke of Wellington"), but the melody drifts into the key of D minor, bringing to mind the myth of Troutbeck and the sadness of willow trees.

Grandioso opens Chinese fortune cookies. None of the messages assuage his sorrow, and without giving any thought to his action he throws the crumbs to the ducks. His idle gesture accomplishes a miracle. The crumbs restore one of the ducks to her true form as Seraphina, the tragic Lady of the Tidal Basin, who rises majestically from the water in a gown of white damask, holding the invincible dragon sword believed to have been lost by John Wayne in a stagecoach accident in Benedict Canyon. Seraphina presents the sword to the astonished Grandioso, explaining as she does so ("Ecco, *Farfalla*") that it cost $32 million and was thrice blessed by Charlton Heston. The emboldened Grandioso seizes the sword and rushes offstage to renew his attack on Malocchio.

INTERLUDE FOR THE CORPS DE BALLET

Reunited with Bearpaw and the forest partisans, Grandioso shuts down the operations of the federal government. The dancers mime the functions of the Mint, the Post Office, the Department of Agriculture, and one by one, as Grandioso strikes them with the invincible dragon sword, they stop moving.

SCENE 5
—*The office of the Speaker of the
House of Representatives, a year later*

The coup d'état has failed, and once again Grandioso has been disgraced. Malocchio continues to play him for a fool, and Gwendolyn the Good no longer hears in his voice the sound of trumpets. The music wanders around in the registers of German despair as Grandioso sings the haunting aria "Why Won't They Let Me Lead?" He looks for comfort to the dead shibboleths mounted on the walls. He has slain so many of them, tracked them through the wilderness of the *New York Times*, brought them down at conference centers, cut their throats on C-SPAN. How is it possible that nobody noticed? Why has it not occurred to the friends of Moth (*Gli Illuminati*) to invest him with the powers and divinities of a philosopher king?

A loud knocking on the door interrupts Grandioso's elegiac monologue. Ringwort and Balthazar burst into the room with great news. They have just come from the House of Scolds (*Das Scheltenhaus*), and they know that God is just. Malocchio has ravaged Fidelia, the fair maid of Rodeo Drive, and the citizenry clamors for revenge. Together with Grandioso, Ringwort and Balthazar sing a jubilant reprise of "I Never Thought I'd See This Day."

## SCENE 6
### *—Noon, the Jefferson Memorial*

The hour of judgment is at hand, and the scene is large and festive. Acrobats, happy villagers, handsome cavalry officers, buxom peasant girls, children rolling hoops. The best people in Washington stand around at stage left, drinking champagne, exchanging hearty gusts of ribald laughter. Balthazar strums Ronald Reagan's magic zither, Grandioso fires Teddy Roosevelt's target pistol, Moth proposes a toast and bravely smashes his glass against a marble column.

Suddenly in the distance we hear the high clear note of a single *Waldhorn*, announcing the approach of doom. As the crowd falls silent the carnival music subsides into a sinister murmuring of cellos, and the palace castrati drag Malocchio onto the stage in a tumbrel. He stands with his hands tied behind his back, but he has lost nothing of his feckless and buoyant spirit. He winks bawdily at Angelina, the unwed gypsy mother, and we know that were it not for the rope on his wrists, he would be off among the peasant women like a beagle chasing squirrels.

The trial takes place at the stone altar in the center of the stage. Der Meisterschelter presides. A basso profundo wearing the costume of a seventeenth-century Puritan clergyman, he sings, a cappella and for two hours, the beloved fulmination *"Tu Sei un Cane Sporco."* The lyrics fall on the head of the evil prince without visible effect. Given a chance to defend his honor, Malocchio sings a nursery rhyme remembered from his childhood in an Arkansas gambling den, *"La Fortuna è Sempre Con Me."* A magistrate asks for a verdict—first from the high-born lords and gracious ladies, then from the happy villagers.

The splendid people jeer and mock and point their jeweled fingers, and among all their glittering company only the Duke of Revlon, the noble Moor, comes forward to sing a rebuttal to the charge of treason, *"Lascia Che il Cane Mangia."* For a long moment it looks as if the evil prince must suffer an evil fate. Grandioso smirks. Rubato gloats. Bearpaw stabs another well-wisher whom he mistakes for Dan Rather.

But when the magistrate puts the question to the common people, they forgive Malocchio. The common people like evil princes; they hope he will bless their crops and look favorably upon their daughters. A court jester unbinds Malocchio's wrists, Grandioso retires in confusion, and the corps de ballet dances the rite of eternal spring. The scene ends as it began—acrobats, carnival music, children rolling hoops.

### SCENE 7
*—The lawn behind the Jefferson*
*Memorial, twenty minutes later*

The fierce partisans have lost the appeal to conscience, and they search for The Five Basic Principles, The Three Essential Reasons. Bearpaw stabs Grandioso, Grandioso stabs Balthazar, Balthazar stabs Ringwort, Ringwort stabs Cobweb, Cobweb stabs Bearpaw. Moth proposes a toast and bravely smashes his glass on Balthazar's Viking helmet.

Beadle returns with his owl, and together they carry off the wounded Grandioso, declaiming a reprise of the recitativo "The Ideas Are Too Big, the Issues Too Important."

### SCENE 8
*—Twilight, the forest on*
*Kennesaw Mountain*

Grandioso enters alone, leading his horse. Once or twice he looks back over his shoulder at the burning city of Rome, but we know by his imbecile grin that he no longer cares for the trifles of Mammon. He has found inner peace and spiritual contentment, and as he climbs higher up the mountain toward the old partisan campfire, he begins to sing, faintly at first but then in a stronger voice and with the accumulating support of more instruments and brighter harmonies, "I Am the Duke of Wellington."

He is far from the tumult of politics, far from Balthazar's maps and the intrigues of Moth, and there is nobody to join him on his march. Nobody but the little woodland folk—the timid rabbit, the shy chipmunk, the cheerful sparrow—who gradually emerge from the forest as Grandioso mounts ever nearer to the sky. They align themselves in military formation, intrepid in the fading light. We hear a chorus of soprano voices, and we know that Grandioso has recruited another army of the faithful, that his song can never die.

*—Full orchestra with brass choir*
*Curtain*

*January 1999*

# Eyebrow Pencils

If one wishes to know the real power of the press, one should
pay attention, not to what it says, but to the way in which it is
listened to. . . . It only cries so loud because its audience is
becoming deaf.
—ALEXIS DE TOCQUEVILLE

Advance copies of John F. Kennedy Jr.'s new political
magazine, *George*, appeared on the New York publicity
circuit in early September, addressed by its founding
editor to the kind of people (very upscale, very hip) apt to think—
at least until they meet *George*—that politics are boring and nasty
and old. The introductory press conference took place in Federal
Hall, in the rotunda where George Washington (the magazine's
namesake and totem) delivered his first inaugural address in the
spring of 1789. Smiling and at ease in the company of both the
dim past and the shiny present, Kennedy greeted the assembled
gossip columnists and television cameras by saying, "I don't think
that I have seen as many of you in one place since they announced
the results of my first bar exams."

His magazine looked a good deal like *Vanity Fair* or *Vogue* (280 glossy pages, delicately scented with an assortment of French perfumes), and in response to questions from the two or three skeptics in the crowd, Kennedy explained (as he also explained in the prefatory note to his 500,000 prospective readers) that *George* was a political magazine from which the politics had been tactfully removed, "a lifestyle magazine" refreshingly devoid of ideas and unencumbered by "any partisan perspective—not even mine," a magazine not unlike a merchandising catalogue "exuberantly" and "extravagantly" bent on exhibiting political figures as "pop icons" and made to the measure of sophisticated consumers certain to bring to their reading of the Bill of Rights or a speech by Bob Dole the same standards of judgment (discriminating) and taste (exquisite) that they bring to their appreciation of an Armani suit, a pair of Ferragamo shoes, or a Louis Vuitton suitcase.

Consistent with the task at hand, the inaugural issue achieved its most striking effects with the advertising: 175 pages of stylish photographs representing all the great and glorious names in the retail merchants' Hall of Fame, not only Armani and Ferragamo but also Tommy Hilfiger, Clinique, Ralph Lauren, Versace, Piaget, Nautica, Valentino, and Donna Karan—the immortals bringing the gifts of the Magi to a cradle of democracy.

The editorial drift of the magazine was coordinated with the advertising copy—Cindy Crawford on the cover as George Washington (noble stance, white powdered wig, eighteenth-century American military uniform, bare midriff, satin ruffle); Cindy Crawford on page 12 (in red silk on behalf of Revlon's "Fire and Ice"); Cindy Crawford on page 210 telling women in Washington how to dress ("If I were first lady, I'd only wear black," "Don't get the cheap panty hose," "Tipper's hair is working"). The bulk of the magazine's prose offered a series of variations on the same tone of voice: up front, under the rubric "Primaries," a few words about George Washington ("[He] was a big man—big hands, big feet, big chest"); chatty pieces about the swell parties attended by the swell new Republican operatives in Washington ("refined strategy sessions for elite leaders" in "genteel" town houses); an account of Julia Roberts on tour among widows and orphans in Haiti (how Julia suffered at the hands of the cruel news media and how her good intentions were rewarded by a waif who said to her, "You're here because you love us"); JFK Jr. himself interviewing George Wallace, the once-upon-a-time racist and governor of Alabama (something of a *tour de force* because the governor is now both deaf and mute); an endpaper entitled "If I Were President," in which Madonna confesses that "I'd rather eat glass" because as president "one day you wake up and find out that you don't have a point of view or a set of balls"; a lead essay "The Next American Revolution Is Now") in which the novelist Caleb Carr promotes the new American political season in language suitable to a report from Paris on the autumn clothes, informing the friends of *George* that when they really stop to think about "all the great issues and events of our day," they, too, will discover what he and John F. Kennedy Jr. and Isaac Mizrahi and Newt Gingrich's lesbian half-sister and Liz Claiborne and Gianfranco Ferre already know: that politics are where it's at.

\*     \*     \*

But if politics were where it's at, who would have time for *George*—a political magazine without the politics and with a fashion model for its muse of fire? Why write letters to the editor with an eyebrow pencil? The questions kept coming to mind as I made my way through the text, and by the time I reached the last four-color photograph (of Madonna swallowing a goldfish) I understood that the magazine would have been more appropriately dedicated to the sacred memory of George III. Here was an expensive collection of celebrities fetchingly arranged in the homespun poses of democratic self-government, but who were the people whom *George* was meant to astonish or impress, and where was the audience for a magazine presenting as its chief virtue the great news that it had nothing to say?

Politics are by definition partisan, because they constitute an argument about power—about who gets to do what to whom, under what circumstances, and for how long and with what degrees of objection or consent. Castrate the quarrel, divorce politics from any meaning that cannot be sold in Wal-Mart, and what is left except a round of applause for William Kristol's tie and Cindy Crawford's hair?

Kennedy, in his prefatory note, speaks of a "freshly engaged public" and a boisterous crowd of presumptive readers "energized by their anger" and eager to indulge "their passion for politics." He might as well have been referring to the immense crowd of well-adjusted and perfectly conditioned people on Planet Reebok. During the 1994 election—the one that all the swell people in the first issue of *George* were talking about as the Second Coming of Christ the Republican—no more than 39 percent of the electorate turned up at the polls, and of those who did, only 25 percent knew the names of their senators or representatives. The country's genuinely political journals circulate among small numbers of readers, and few television public affairs programs command audiences large enough to qualify for a single ratings point. I don't know what kind of crowds the editors of *George* encounter on the great American plains, but in my own wanderings around the country over the last several years I've noticed that without the backing of the Christian Coalition or the addition of large celebrity (personages on the order of Elizabeth Taylor or Henry Kissinger) political meetings tend to consist of twenty or thirty people whose hair isn't working, seated on folding chairs in a small room, asking questions either bitterly partisan, hopelessly irrelevant, or terminally paranoid—studio audiences sometimes positioned for the C-SPAN cameras to suggest the illusion of a quorum.

The general lack of interest in political affairs corresponds to the general disaffection for anything and everything modified by the adjective "public." For twenty years the drum majors of the Republican parade band have been beating time to the same ideological refrain—private schools, private prisons, private suburbs, private roads, private money, private police—and by now even the crippled remnant of the Democratic Party has come to acknowledge the sovereignty of private means over public ends. All things bright and beautiful flow forth from the clear mountain streams of the private sector; all things vicious and ugly rise from the swamp of the public sector. Power derives its legitimacy and authority from the mints of private wealth, not from the coinage of public thought, and people who once might have thought of themselves as citizens now tend to think of themselves as the vassals of a commercial overlord.

Corporations of the magnitude of IBM or Citibank constitute themselves as what Renaissance Europe would have recognized as city-states, sovereign powers employing as many people as once lived in Philadelphia in 1789. When it suits their interests, they send their agents to Congress (as they did last spring with respect to the telecommunications and environmental bills) to write the necessary laws. A man without a company name is a man without a country; it is no longer the political commonwealth that furnishes him with a pension, medical insurance, club membership, credit cards, meaning, and a common store of experience. As recently as a hundred years ago most Americans lived in small towns arranged around a public square or green, a community consisting of a school, a courthouse, and a church, and our range of observation was available free of charge. Now we must pay for what goes by the name of common experience at the stadium, the cineplex, or the mall, and we define ourselves as the sum of our possessions or the collection of our ticket stubs.

*George* proceeds from the assumption that the important political decisions take place in private (at the Federal Reserve Board, on one of the Bechtel Corporation's airplanes, over breakfast at the Willard Hotel), that what Versace has to say (even in Italian) is a good deal more interesting than who gets elected president of the United States or what the Congress says to itself about the balanced budget or the war in Bosnia. But in the meantime somebody has to keep up appearances, maintain the fiction of a national political debate, make lists of Senator Alfonse D'Amato's favorite songs and pasta dishes, organize the props and lights for what John F. Kennedy Jr. (again in his prefatory note and attributing his insight to his lifelong access to the best seats in the American grandstand) calls "the giant puppet show that can turn public people into barely recognizable symbols of themselves."

On or about the same day that Kennedy introduced his new magazine to the ladies and gentlemen of the press in Federal Hall, General Colin Powell set forth on a twenty-five-city tour to promote his autobiography, *My American Journey*, and the two events were as well matched as Cindy Crawford's accessories—a political campaign that wasn't a political campaign, a post-partisan candidate refreshingly devoid of controversial views, a politician from whom the politics had been tactfully removed, a fall fashion statement (noble stance, twentieth-century military uniform, firm jaw, many medals) made to fit the cover of everybody's magazine. The news media hustled the general into the limelight with the effusive haste of a starving mob in a besieged city welcoming the arrival of a relief column. The country was said to be in desperate straits, exhibiting ominous signs of moral rot and social decay, and here at hand was a great captain embodying all the old-time American virtues believed to have gone AWOL from a Saigon bar in the summer of 1969. Within a matter of a few days in September, Powell appeared before the talk-show cameras with Barbara Walters and Jay Leno, *Time* magazine published a 7,500-word excerpt from the Random House book (500,000 copies shipped,

$6 million author's advance), and newspaper columnists of all per-
suasions abandoned themselves to a frenzy of praise—"classic
soldier-statesman," "a president for all seasons," "transcends
politics," "photographic memory." Powell not only was a hero—
a man who had "power-walked" with Presidents Reagan, Bush,
and Clinton—but he was also black, "America's black Eisen-
hower." Not *too* black, of course, not so black that he would scare
anybody, but black enough to stand as a symbol of payment for
a long-overdue debt, allowing white people to imagine—at least
for the time being and while being questioned by the opinion
polls—that they were tolerant and kind and wise, so emancipated
from racial prejudice that they could seriously entertain the prospect of a black man in the White House.

In the small print behind the dress uniform and the glittering
adjectives, the general didn't quite come up to the promise of the
ad copy. A deft and self-promoting careerist, he apparently had
risen through the ranks by never doing or saying anything that
ruffled the surface of the consensus already present in the briefing
room, an officer so disinclined to take risks that he worked out a
doctrine of guaranteed victory, committing the United States
Army only to those wars that it could easily win (preferably in
deserts, never in mountains), a military bureaucrat so skilled in
the arts of camouflage that in Vietnam in 1968 he adroitly delayed
discovery of the My Lai massacre, a policy operative so sinuous
that when in Washington in 1986 as the Assistant Secretary of
Defense administered the illegal transfer of arms to Iran, he
blandly failed to recall (114 times) any knowledge of the event at
the subsequent congressional hearings—in brief and in sum, an

accommodating man who once told the *Washington Post* that "issues come and go" but "process" lives forever.

Nor did his book, or at least those fragments of it that I read in *Time*, contradict the impression of a latter-day Polonius. The general told the story of his life as a series of uplifting homilies consistent with the plotlines of television situation comedy— strong family ties, up from poverty in the South Bronx by dint of good conduct and hard work, off to the army, which he embraced as "my home . . . my life . . . my love," aide-de-camp to a series of important people in and around the White House, lots of power-walking, chairman of the Joint Chiefs of Staff. On the questions that threatened to veer off into the swamp of politics, the general let issues come and go and stayed steadfastly with process. Yes, he had "Republican leanings," but he was also "a New Deal kid"—conservative but not too conservative, a believer in "discipline" but also a strong supporter of "compassion," vague about abortion and capital gains taxes, solidly in favor of mother and the flag.

Reading the general's text, I remembered having once been told that during the fall of 1941, when German tanks had advanced to within ten miles of Moscow, the managers of the Soviet Union placed a wax dummy of Joseph Stalin in a lighted window of the Kremlin, high enough up off the street to escape close inspection but near enough to sustain the illusion of a godlike presence. Stalin the man might have been in a bomb shelter or the Crimea, but Stalin the wax figure, tireless in his labors and impervious to fear, remained stolidly at his post, the great leader alone in his study, seated calmly at his desk, directing the armies in the field, and summoning from the impregnable soil of Mother Russia the strength of 10,000 armored divisions.

The United States in the autumn of 1995 isn't as badly off as Moscow in October 1941, but still it is a comfort to see Colin Powell and Cindy Crawford high up in the lighted windows of the news media and to know that if they really put their minds to it, either singly or together, they could probably summon from the pages of the imperishable American past the mighty spirit ("big hands, big feet, big chest") of *George*.

*November 1995*

# Asset Management

Nothing makes one so vain as being told that one is a sinner.
—OSCAR WILDE

*F*or quite a few years now the business media have been touting the wisdom of what they call "trimming out the fat," and although I never know precisely what the phrase means—why the incompetent chairman retires with an honorarium of $50 million while 20,000 of his former employees receive notices of dismissal—I understand the general principle. Money attaches itself to velocity, and a successful corporation cannot afford to carry around excess weight. The competition is too fierce, the markets too volatile, the new technologies as fast-moving as cancer cells. The chairman's $50 million weighs practically nothing—a row of numbers on a computer screen, a handful of credit cards, maybe a gold watch as thin as the wing of a moth. The 20,000 employees, on the other hand, require heavy maintenance and take up too much storage space, also too much light and air. They stand in the way of progress and block the view of the future.

Not unlike a chorus of press agents promoting a spa in Arizona, the corporate spokespersons announcing the merger of companies extol the wonders of benign subtraction—"streamlining" the distribution systems, "downsizing" the workforce, "eliminating redundancy." Similar messages show up most everywhere else in a society devoted to the causes of comfort and convenience. Four-color illustrations in the women's magazines recommend the glamorous paring down of one's diet, thighs, and living-room furniture; telephone and cable television services work toward a single strand of fiber-optic glass bearing the burden of all the words in all the books in all the world's libraries; fashion designers find the ideal form of feminine beauty in runway models reduced to minimalist silhouettes, as light as political campaign promises, as disposable as paper towels.

A trend so firmly established does not brook contradiction, and over the next twenty years we no doubt can expect to see the strategies of merger and simplification applied to the Western cultural and intellectual tradition. Too many outworn ideas clutter the attic of civilization with premises no longer valid, and structures of thought once splendid in the light of a fifth-century morning or a nineteenth-century afternoon (Arthurian legend, Ptolemaic astronomy, Marxist socioeconomic theory) stand around in the corners with the Roman swords and medieval suits of armor. Most of the scientific scribblings haven't weathered the storms of time, but several of the philosophical and religious propositions retain elements of meaning that might be made to fit our own modern predicament. Properly restructured, of course, and with a sharp eye for trimming out the fat.

Because the heaviest weights of paper and the largest collections of art owe their existence to the inspiration of the Christian Church, the new management team might wish to make a beginning with the concepts of Heaven and Hell. Quite clearly we no longer need both establishments, each with its own procedures and tables of organization, its own letterhead, advertising budget, and mission statement. At the behest of President Ronald Reagan, Heaven relocated its headquarters to America in the winter of 1983, and it doesn't make much sense to continue to fund a gated community only slightly superior to the ones in Florida and California—the destination within easy reach of the commercial airlines, the doorkeepers glad to accept all the major credit cards.

Eliminating the redundancy of Heaven forces the question about whether to retain the seven cardinal virtues or the seven deadly sins. Which isn't to say that the virtues won't be missed. Always admirable and unfailingly welcome in commencement speeches, they add an atmosphere of old-world charm to any boardroom or Senate office in which their framed portraits hang quietly on the walls. But they don't meet the requirements of the global market. Impossible to sell in large volume and serving no purpose at White House dinners, the virtues remain hard to practice either in their classical forms (wisdom, courage, temperance, and justice) or under their Christian names (faith, hope, and charity).

The sins speak more directly to the emotions and the whims of the moment, and it is on the sins, singly or in synergetic combination, that a consumer society depends for its amusement and 95 percent of its gross domestic product. They aren't as much fun as the virtues, and they don't provide their constituents with anywhere near the same degrees of freedom (either of body or mind), but they are very good for business. The sins in all their denominations (venal as well as mortal) sustain the volume in the stock market, employ the otherwise unemployable, excite the fevers of speculation, stimulate the passions for sexual and political novelty. Trim out the fat of the seven virtues, and nothing bad happens to the price of real estate or the Dow Jones Industrial Average; take away the seven deadly sins, and the country goes promptly broke.

And yet, despite their many valuable contributions to society over the last 1,500 years, the sins continue to attract a good deal of adverse criticism, some of it warranted but much of it intemperate and ungrateful. The medieval schoolmen can be forgiven their diatribes because they didn't live in a consumer society, and they didn't understand that temptation is the blessed state of being that generates sales. Modern critics familiar with the revelations of John Maynard Keynes (also with the miracles in the desert of unlimited credit) cannot plead the same excuse. Their attachment to sentimental metaphor binds them to the rhetoric of the past, to a mercantile rather than a capitalist view of human desire, and they fail to see that the sins—when properly appreciated as the mainsprings of social progress—incorporate the functions of the virtues.

## PRIDE

Leave vanity out of the equation and who would run the government or the Bank of America? What politician would stand for public office? Who would paint another toenail or sing another song?

The old preachers dwelled at length on the evils of self-love and self-promotion, assigning traits of character to a puff of Dutch velvet or a scrap of Spanish lace. More often than not they mistook the ornament for the man, and they discounted the uses of vainglory as a cure for bad conscience and the best of remedies against the awful recognition of one's own weakness, stupidity, and fear.

Left to its own devices and unencumbered by sermons, pride accomplishes the tasks of charity. University presidents offer "naming opportunities" to wealthy patrons who bestow the gifts of libraries and football stadiums. Were it not for at least some small measure of pride, why else would Ted Turner give $1 billion to the United Nations or Bill Gates set aside the same amount for the education of proud, well-deserving college students?

Pride goeth before destruction, but destruction sells cosmetics, aircraft carriers, and newspapers.

## COVETOUSNESS

The collapse of Soviet Communism can be read as a parable about what happens to a society that seeks to banish the sin of covetousness. Poorly informed critics, most of them foreigners or leftists, fail to notice that among American consumers the acts of getting and spending serve a spiritual, not a material, purpose. The faithful regard the rights of purchase as the proofs of grace, and they go shopping in much the same way that medieval pilgrims stopped to pray at wayside shrines. The transaction brings with it a presentiment of everlasting bliss, also the comfort of having acknowledged the perfection of the supernatural design.

Similar to the rite of communion, the rituals of consumption partake of the body and blood of divinity, and the more costly the substance consumed—a dress by Valentino, an ounce of Peruvian cocaine, a three-month cruise around the world priced at $265,000—the more perfectly the communicant enters into a union with the invisible hand of God. Because nothing is superfluous and everything counts (yea, even to the least of chocolate-covered hazelnuts and the sayings of Newt Gingrich), the consumption of cheap toys and low-end pornography becomes an act of piety as devout as the buying of a Gulfstream IV or a president of the United States.

## ANGER AND LUST

The twin glories of the news and entertainment business. Suppress either one of them in favor of their virtuous antonyms—i.e., with the peace that passeth all understanding and the chastity of Snow White—and the great American television audience would rise in open rebellion. The National Football League would depart into bankruptcy, taking with it the fashion industry, large sectors of the legal profession, the manufacturers of soap and automobiles who package their products with the pornographic images that sell the services and move the goods. The few journalists still at large might learn to content themselves with making lists of yesterday's temperature readings, but in the houses of Congress the politicians would have nothing to say to one another; neither would the actors in the World Wrestling Federation or the characters in the novels of Danielle Steel.

## GLUTTONY

The supreme law of the consumer society holds that nobody ever has enough, and America's sustained prosperity follows from a general sense of unassuaged emptiness and perpetual discontent. The doctrine of rugged individualism presupposes an insatiable appetite ("Be All You Can Be," "You Can Have It All"), and whenever the economy runs into sufficiently serious trouble, the authorities in New York and Washington prescribe the same remedy—place enough cash in the hands of the American consumers, and they will stampede through the world's markets like a herd of famished buffalo, setting in motion the happy sequence of events that leads to more spending, more investment, more confidence, more traffic deaths, more missiles, more amphetamines.

Understood as indomitable courage and unbounded optimism, the voraciousness of the American appetite guarantees the safety of the free world; were it not for our steadfast buying of European luxury goods and cheap Chinese labor (the annual trade deficit currently estimated at $300 billion), the armies of Slobodan Milosevic and Saddam Hussein would be standing at the gates of Paris.

## ENVY

A theoretically egalitarian society that invites all of its citizens to compete on the same footing for the same inventories of reward sets up a market for demonstrable inequality. The market trades in the currencies of envy, which increase the rates of expenditure in the showrooms of self-esteem for people who fix their self-worth by the degrees of their association with private schools, exclusive clubs, precious brand names.

Understood not as a sin but as a system of measurement or a means of education, envy sharpens the powers of observation, exercises the memory, teaches arithmetic. Celebrity biographies take the place of the lives of the saints.

## SLOTH

Although preserved as a sin in the Christian scheme of things, sloth in a consumer society expresses the virtues of temperance and humility. Seated placidly on a couch in front of the television set, the ideal American citizen can muster just enough energy to change the channel and push the buttons that bring the diamond from the shopping network, order the pizza and the *Playboy* movie, answer yes or no to the questions on an opinion poll. The habit of mind promotes political stability and nurtures the body of ideal citizens not likely to incite a riot or quarrel with the police.

Space doesn't permit detailed analysis of all the advantages sure to follow from the merging of the virtues with the sins; the organizers of the new and much simplified Web site undoubtedly will find other vocabularies that can be discarded, other ways to streamline the real estate development of Heaven on earth, more fat to trim. The cost savings should prove significant.

The keeping track of answered and unanswered prayers can be outsourced to the Bahamas; the angels, all of them remarkably good-looking people, should have no trouble finding work as headwaiters in New York restaurants, lap dancers in Las Vegas, personal trainers in Beverly Hills.

*November 1999*

# *Natural Selection*

American Talent Management
1504 Sunset Boulevard
West Hollywood, CA 90069

May 20, 2000

Ms. Vivian Taylor
461 Eucalyptus Drive
Cupertino, CA 95015

Dear Ms. Taylor,

American Talent Management doesn't make promises, but I believe that we can do something for little Leslie. She's a beautiful child, as appealing a six-year-old girl as any of us here remember ever having seen, and I can think of no reason why she shouldn't become a headline name.

As you undoubtedly will have guessed, a lot of parents come to us with large ambitions for their children, but it isn't often that we send them contracts. Leslie is one of the rare exceptions, fortunate not only in her blonde hair and angelic smile but also, if you'll allow me to say so, in her mother's appreciation of the ways in which the entertainment business has changed since the days when Judy Garland was singing "Over the Rainbow." When you brought Leslie and her canary into the office last Tuesday for her audition with the television camera, you didn't ask us to watch her tap-dance, and everybody in the meeting was impressed by your sense of what interests the producers who book the acts on *60 Minutes* and CNN.

None of us doubts that Leslie was born to be a star. She's as wonderful on camera as JonBenet Ramsey, and her poise is truly remarkable. We asked her to talk to her canary as if she were talking to Barbara Walters, and you will notice that at no point in the interview is she at a loss for an adorable answer.

I enclose the videocassette together with our contract, and I think you'll be pleased by Leslie's command of the talk-show language. You have a credible daughter, Ms. Taylor, but, as you also must know, we're dealing in a perishable good. Youth is a precious commodity, and when we spoke about the news media devoting twice as much time and space to Elián González as to either John F. Kennedy Jr. or Princess Di, I didn't have to tell you that we must gather our rosebuds while we may. Leslie's contract expires on her eleventh birthday, the age at which young girls begin to run away to the circus of adult entertainment.

Twenty or thirty years ago we might have placed Leslie in a soap commercial as well as in the Rose Bowl parade as a dancing flower, but the trend in advertising these days favors high-speed visual effects, hard-edged and ironic. Nor do we have much chance with the movie studios. The sought-after directors in town look for kids with empty faces and dead eyes. Their films send messages about our postmodern descent into barbarism, and they put out casting calls for children who fit the specifications for the monstrous and grotesque—deaf-mutes, victims of drug and sexual abuse, small psychopaths. You and I both know that the movies are unfair and untrue, but we live with a box office transformed in ways that we might not always wish, and for Leslie at the moment the most we could expect would be a cameo role as the symbol of lost innocence, the little girl in the wrong place at the wrong time, pushed off a cliff in the opening sequence that tells the audience to expect grim but important lessons.

American Talent Management doesn't flatter its clients with false hopes—you also will have noticed the clause in the contract about your own appearance on *Who Wants to Be a Millionaire*—but we need to be clear about our objectives. What we have is a market for "reality," for strong material that works better in a headline than a theater. The news media feed the appetites of an audience increasingly dissatisfied with the flow of make-believe blood, and their competition for product obeys Darwin's rule about the survival of the fittest.

We already have pitched Leslie to the producers of the CBS show that strands sixteen people on an uninhabited island in the South China Sea. They liked the idea, liked Leslie's attitude and the video, but we were too late. The cast was en route to Borneo. Several other possibilities still in early development suggest that the European craze for reality-based programming has found its way to Hollywood. NBC is said to be thinking about sending a Boy Scout troop to Kosovo, and ABC has expressed interest in the sale of young American girls to rich businessmen in Asia. What the scriptwriters apparently have in mind is a game show that combines the glamour of the Miss America Pageant with the excitement of an antiques auction and the romance of the old Roman slave trade. The Sultan of Brunei has indicated a preference for California blondes slightly older than Leslie (slightly older and not quite as fragile), but we think the network people will see that the lower age translates into higher rating points.

Strong material entails a certain degree of risk, Vivian, but the rewards are correspondingly great, and on Tuesday everybody was glad to hear you say of Leslie that she was "a little trooper." Assuming that we bring your daughter safely back to the studio of *Good Morning America*, she sits on the floor with Diane Sawyer and explains the mysteries of the Orient to the Sock Puppet and a jury of anatomically correct dolls.

We also have notions of our own, and some stories needn't be left to chance. You can help provide a home environment hospitable to the accidents of fame by removing the V-chips from the television sets in the basement, by encouraging her to explore the pornographic headwaters of the Internet, and by taking her on more frequent visits to her father in prison. You said you planned to travel to Israel in the autumn, and we know people on the Palestinian side of the politics who want to buy into the American media industry. If we can work out the distribution deal for the eventual miniseries, they might agree to abduct the little trooper

from the terrace of the King David Hotel. For every day she stays
in the tents of the terrorists, we bring down another zero to the
bottom line.

I mention the Jerusalem scenario because you already have the
plane tickets, but equally good opportunities present themselves
almost everywhere else in the remote parts of the world. Rebel
armies roam the streets in most of the capital cities of Africa, and
if nothing comes of the trip to Israel we can talk about sending
Leslie to see the sunsets in Angola or Sierra Leone. Or maybe she
somehow falls into the Caribbean Sea, five miles off the coast of
Colombia on Christmas morning, with an inner tube and a pair
of dolphins from the Miami Seaquarium. Four drug dealers bound
for Panama with 150 kilos of cocaine show up half an hour later
in a passing cigarette boat, but as soon as they see the dolphins
they know they're looking at a miracle. They jettison their evil
cargo to make room for a messenger from God. The fisherfolk in
Cartagena see Leslie as an incarnation of the Virgin Mary, and for
the next five months they refuse to send her home to Cupertino.

You don't need American Talent Management to add up the
score in market share. What we have is a page one political crisis,
possibly a guest appearance by the United States Navy, and we
figure that most of the risk is in the water on day one. Even the
best of drug dealers can't be relied upon to arrive on cue, and so
we're taking the chance that maybe the little trooper drowns. Your
kind of bet, Vivian, a lot better than a lottery ticket and the odds
no worse than a twenty to one horse at the track at San Diego.

*     *     *

While we were waiting for the elevator after the meeting on Tuesday, you mentioned your own three marriages and Leslie's dysfunctional home life. Let me assure you that nothing has been lost. A good many of our younger clients come from dysfunctional families (as do many of our most beloved celebrities and well-known politicians), and their experience almost always adds an element of melodrama to the story and sets up the moralizing columnists with trenchant proofs for their general theory of American decadence. Think of Leslie's father as a hidden asset. A lot of Vietnam War veterans weren't very good about controlling their rage, and you remember the court psychiatrist saying that Ellis's attempt to dynamite the Golden Gate Bridge was a "not entirely irrational act of rebellion." The psychiatrist wasn't as sanguine about the six Chinese cooks Ellis killed after he lost $500 in a mahjong game, but if his daughter becomes famous G. Gordon Liddy will find extenuating circumstances, and we can anticipate well-publicized protests meant to secure his release from prison.

Does Leslie know how to handle firearms? If not, we might want to consider hiring a tutor. Another preparation for the unexpected turning of fortune's wheel. Ellis presumably left a small-caliber pistol lying around the house that the police neglected to confiscate, and you might find one under the kitchen sink.

From what you told us about Leslie's public school, I don't imagine that it's an especially safe place. Sooner or later we can expect trouble, and on the lucky day when two alienated students show up in Nazi uniforms with a manifesto and semi-automatic rifles, Leslie shoots them down like dogs. A great story, Vivian, and one to which American Talent Management would be proud to lend a helping hand. Let the incident occur in late October, and I can see your daughter testifying before Congress and Larry King, Leslie on the White House lawn, Leslie the star of both presidential election campaigns.

The more I think about Leslie as a property the more I like her in the role of the little girl who saves the day. Another agency might advise you to play it the other way—Leslie shooting her gym teacher, Leslie busting her father out of San Quentin—but although those stories make excellent copy, they don't help build a career. They are not heartwarming stories, Vivian, and they seldom last much longer than a week. Don't listen to consultants who tell you otherwise. They might offer to take a smaller percentage, but they don't have Leslie's best interests at heart. Read our contract carefully and you will see that it awards you a generous share of the posthumous subsidiary rights.

Which isn't to say that you shouldn't continue Leslie's voice and ballet lessons together with her weapons training. In show business nobody ever knows what's coming next, and if George Bush wins the election in November maybe we'll find ourselves in a market for spelling bees and banjo music.

Once you have reviewed the terms of our agreement we'll set up another meeting; in the meantime please say hello to Leslie's canary and give the little trooper the safari hat as a token of our affection and esteem.

Yours sincerely,
Howard Fineman

*July 2000*

# Fatted Calf

Oh, Mother! I was born to die soon;
but Olympian Zeus the Thunderer
owes me some honor for it.
ACHILLES, IN THE *ILIAD*

Diana, Princess of Wales, died in Paris shortly before dawn on August 31, and less than an hour later in Cape Town, South Africa, heralds of the Olympian news media appealed to her brother, Charles Edward Maurice, 9th Earl Spencer, for a sound bite of farm-fresh grief. Lord Spencer didn't read from the standard script. Instead of supplying the hoped-for sentiment, he said he always knew that "the press would kill her in the end," and then, not yet satisfied with what seemed too plain and obvious a statement, he went on to say that ". . . every proprietor and editor of every publication that has paid for intrusive and exploitative photographs of her, encouraging greedy and ruthless individuals to risk everything in pursuit of Diana's image, has blood on their hands today."

The rebuke had a fine, Victorian ring to it, but it presupposed an order of meaning and a system of communication as far behind the times as the court protocol of the British monarchy. Had the earl been talking to Rudyard Kipling or Henry James, one or both gentlemen might have presented an apology. But he was talking to television cameras, which have as little interest in the uses of civility as a mob of voracious gulls. His sister was a celebrity, and celebrities are consumer products meant to be consumed.

The earl had once worked as a correspondent for NBC, and he would have known that in London and Paris and New York, the news media already had begun to cut and paste his dead sister into strips of videotape and fillets of print. He would have guessed at the frenzy of the assignment editors reaching for the phones, the excitement of the special-effects people composing the computer graphic of the accident in the tunnel under the Place de l'Alma, the anticipation of thrilling news among the technicians setting up the camera angles at Kensington Palace and The Mall.

Maybe the earl also remembered something of his reading of the Homeric poems. He attended Eton and Oxford, two schools still acquainted with the study of classical antiquity, and it's conceivable that he had in mind a sacrificial feast not unlike the one that Nestor, king in Pylos, dedicated to the worship of Zeus's daughter, bright-eyed Pallas Athena. As described in the third book of the Odyssey, the ritual required the slaughter of "a yearling heifer/broad in the brow, unbroken, never yoked by men." Nestor instructs his goldsmith, skilled Laerces, to "come and sheathe the heifer's horns in gold," and then, after pouring the lustral water and scattering the barley meal, the women shrill their cry, and noble Pisistratus slashes the heifer's throat,

Dark blood gushed forth, life ebbed from her limbs—
they quartered her quickly, cut the thighbones out
and all according to custom wrapped them round in fat,
a double fold sliced clean and topped with strips of flesh.
And the old king burned these over dried split wood
and over the fire poured out glistening wine
while young men at his side held five-pronged forks.
Once they'd burned the bones and tasted the organs,
they sliced the rest into pieces, spitted them on skewers
and raising points to the fire, broiled all the meats.

Which, most things considered and other things being equal, is what became of Diana, Princess of Wales. There were, of course, refinements. Over the last 3,000 years we've improved upon the old ways of broiling the meats and arranging their display and distribution to the suppliants crowding around the blood. The wonders of modern technology make it possible to render the burning of every bone and the tasting of every organ as a sequence of pleasant images rather than as strips of flesh spitted on skewers and five-pronged forks. Skilled Laerces is not one but many, and before noon on the day of the princess's death, a thousand gossip columnists had sheathed her memory in clichés of precious gold; by nightfall the television producers assembling two- and three-hour special programs had wrapped round in fat the pieces of what had been her life—Diana in her wedding carriage, Diana carrying a black child or riding a white horse, Diana triumphant and Diana at bay, Diana in the harbor at Saint-Tropez on an Egyptian's gilded barge; at the hour of the rising moon it remained only for the anchorpersons to step forward into the studio light and pour out the wine of glistening bathos.

All according to custom, accompanied by the music of flutes, and the next morning in London and New York the tabloid press presented the news of Diana's death in a Paris traffic accident as an event comparable to the assassination of President John F. Kennedy or the sinking of the *Titanic*. The upmarket press confirmed the judgment, the *New York Times* devoting 45 percent of its general news space to the story, the *Times* of London twenty of its twenty-eight news pages.

The consumption of the princess's remains preserved the character of a religious festival through the whole of the week preceding the funeral service on September 6 in Westminster Abbey. Other celebrities of approximate magnitude sprinkled the lustral water and scattered the barley meal, again all according to custom in descending order of rank. First Tony Blair, the British prime minister, who was near to weeping when he said of Diana that "she was the people's Princess . . . in our hearts and our memories forever"; then President Clinton laying the wreath of his sorrow before a press conference in Martha's Vineyard; afterward Henry Kissinger, John Travolta, Elizabeth Taylor, and the entire procession of palace sycophants and bereaved fashion-magazine editors brought forward by one or another of the television networks to dip their fingers into the entrails and say, with Lady Thatcher in the *Sun*, that "a beacon of light has been extinguished," with Paul

Johnson in the *Daily Mail*, that "she was a 'gem of purest ray serene,'" or, most simply, with Liz Smith in *Newsday*, "Beyond words. Beyond words." As long as everybody got the tone right, it didn't matter what anybody said, because even the bearers of the most intimate witness were talking not about a human being but about a golden mask behind which they were welcome to imagine the presence of Aphrodite Urania, Queen Elizabeth I, or a neurotic child.

The anchorpersons regulating the flows of insipid recollection invited their studio guests and distant correspondents to savor the choicest cuts of gossip. Five years ago over lunch at the Four Seasons, what was it that the princess had said about bulimia or Valentino's dresses? About her cavalry officer and Prince Charles on the telephone to Camilla Parker Bowles? What would become of the British royal family, those stodgy and unfeeling Germans? Was it true that Dodi was an imbecile, and did she often think of suicide?

During the dull moments, when nothing new was to be learned from the Paris police, or when the program's bookers were having trouble placing the next guest in front of a camera in East Hampton, the networks showed film of the wrecked Mercedes, shrouding it by the end of the week with the mystical significance of O. J. Simpson's Ford Bronco.

On most of the subjects taken up for discussion (Diana's astrologer, Prince Charles's polo ponies and Dodi's toy boats, Diana comforting the rejected and oppressed, why Paris was always the wrong place to be seen in August), most of the participants managed a polite murmuring of pious cant. The only topic that excited all present (anchorperson, bearer of intimate witness, distant watcher in the Brompton Road) to the expression of a firm or indignant opinion was the one about blaming the press for the traffic accident. Was it possible, as Lord Spencer had said, that the press was somehow guilty of a crime?

As probably was to be expected, the most unctuous professions of innocence appeared on ABC, during the broadcast of the first of its special programs addressed to what the network billed as "The Royal Tragedy." The three principals—Diane Sawyer, Peter Jennings, and Barbara Walters—periodically interrupted their complacent sucking of the marrow from the bones of wonderful, wonderful Diana to disapprove, with an air of condescension and disgust, of those awful paparazzi on motorcycles (jackals, shameless vermin, vile scum, beasts) who were no friends of the First Amendment. Peter mentioned ethics. Barbara said, "You know, some people could even accuse you and me, Diane, occasionally, perhaps, of going too far." Diane, quoting a British newspaper, said, "We have rules that govern hunters stalking prey in the forest. Can't we at least offer some peace to the young people who live in the palaces?" Leaning closer to the table and confiding to her co-hosts her deeper knowledge of the paparazzi and their con-temptible motives, Barbara said, sotto voce, "They take money."

So does Barbara; so do the editors of *Newsweek* and *Vogue;* so did everybody else who dined that week on Diana rôti or Diana en croûte, but none of them had the grace to acknowledge their debt to the peasants on black motorcycles who fatten the sacrificial cattle and herd them, squealing, through the streets of Paris or across the hillsides of the Cotswolds and the Côte d'Azur.

\*     \*     \*

Like the making of sausage or violin strings, the minting of celebrity is not a pretty business. The news media affix price tags to the carcasses of temporary divinity, but in return for the gifts of wealth and applause, they require the king of the month or queen for a day to make the remnants of his or her humanity available to the ritual of the public feast. What was once a subject becomes an object—a corporate logo or a T-shirt, a product convenient to a supermarket checkout counter, a brand name capable of awakening with its "personal touch" the spirit dormant in a basketball sneaker or a bottle of perfume.

The bargain is a Faustian one, but not all of the contracts end in bloodshed. Sometimes the individual in question need only consent to a loss of freedom, of speech as well as movement; sometimes it is sufficient merely to submit to one of the several forms of castration and decay that render the celebrity as harmless as a drop-by by Kim Basinger or a song by Barry Manilow. But Diana was a celebrity of the most vulnerable and therefore the most nourishing type, a victim for all seasons whom her brother memorialized in his eulogy as "a very insecure person," marked by her "deep feelings of unworthiness." She accepted the media's terms of cruel endearment with the pathetic gratitude of a born nonentity, avid for the limelight because she hoped to find the needle of her self in the haystack of her press clippings. Together with her brilliant smile and the appearance of having been granted every wish in Aladdin's lamp—youth, beauty, pretty dresses, a prince for a husband, and Elton John for a pet—she projected a

sense of loneliness and loss. Her fans cherished her for her need-
iness, which was as desperate and as formless as their own.

Like the Greek kings in sandy Pylos sacrificing bulls to Posei-
don, the news media hold up to their audiences what their audiences wish to see, and because the television camera invests
authority in feeling instead of thought, the shows of weakness
become the proofs of strength. Divine celebrity stands on the altars
of self-dramatization, and, as the crowds in the London streets
made clear to the Queen of England during the week of Diana's
death and transfiguration, we live in an age that casts the victim
as the hero of the play. Who listens to the stories of people who
don't make of their lives a chronicle of endless woe?

During the last days of her life, the princess apparently wished
to divorce the cameras that always had loved her and that she once
regarded as her lifelong friends. She had as little chance of escape
as a parrot in a cage or an elephant in a zoo. Too many people
had spent too much time and money machine-tooling her persona
for the market in daydreams.

Reading the newspapers on the morning after her funeral, I
tried to recall the names of other twentieth-century celebrities
blown up into balloons of comparable size. It was a short list.
Omitting people famous for their works and deeds as well as for
their images (Elvis Presley, Eva Perón, Jack and Bobby Kennedy),
I counted only the figures who, like Diana, served as pretty pieces
of blank paper on which their fans could draw their own fantastic
scrawls. Within this narrower classification, I noticed that of those
who had been my near contemporaries—Marilyn Monroe, James
Dean, Grace Kelly—the best known died young, and I was sur-

prised to discover that although for periods of ten or fifteen years I must have seen one or another of their photographs five or six times a day, I could remember almost nothing of the fictions that had been their lives. A familiar pose, a song, a scene in a mediocre movie—little else.

Among the persons denominated as celebrities in the earlier years of the twentieth century, Charles Lindbergh most closely resembled Diana, but only in the degree of magnification. Lindbergh didn't accept the bargain offered by the press. He was twenty-five years old when he flew the *Spirit of St. Louis* from New York to Paris in May 1927, but, unlike Diana, he knew how to read the contract guaranteeing the specious promise of immortality. He took off from Roosevelt Field in the rain, an obscure stunt pilot from somewhere in the Midwest with a quart of water and five sandwiches that he had picked up at a diner in Queens; thirty-three and a half hours later he was a demigod alighting on the earth at Le Bourget in a crowd of 100,000 people who knew him as a heaven-sent sign from Zeus, the thunderer. The surge of emotion circled the world like a pulse of light. Cheered by crowds in Paris, and then again by crowds in Brussels and London, Lindbergh returned to America on a cruiser sent by President Coolidge, and the ticker-tape parade in New York was better attended and more tumultuous than the ones celebrating the victories of World War I and II.

For the next few months women embraced him in the streets; laundry men stole his shirts for souvenirs; his bank checks went uncashed because their value was his autograph. Well-wishers in sixty-nine countries sent 15,000 presents—mostly jewels and medals but also a dress sword, a Gutenberg Bible, and a cane carved from a tree in Mark Twain's garden. The manufacturers of celebrity offered movies, newspaper columns, books, a vaudeville act.

Lindbergh took none of the deals, gave the presents to a museum, and learned to avoid photographers. When his child was kidnapped and killed in 1932, he was again hounded by the press in all the ways that have since become familiar to Sly Stallone and Demi Moore. He moved to Europe for four years, long enough for his name to fall out of the newspapers and the mouths of his admirers, but before leaving for his term of exile, he explained his reason for going to a reporter for the *New York Times*: "At first you can stand the spotlight in your eyes. Then it blinds you. Others can see you, but you cannot see them."

Neither could Diana. Nor could the fatted calf in Pylos, blinded by the firelight, startled by the knife.

*November 1997*

# Mixed Media

A work in which there are theories is like an object which still
has its price-tag on it.
—MARCEL PROUST

Although I long ago learned to approach exhibitions of
contemporary American art with the same wariness that
I bring to government press briefings and Protestant
boarding schools, I went to the Whitney Museum in early March
with the faint hope that the passing of the Cold War might have
tempered the native impulse to correct and improve the conscience
of the age. I had no good reason to entertain such a hope, but in
reading the work of some of the younger American writers I had
noticed less of an emphasis on ideological statement and more of
an interest in historical narrative, and I thought it possible that
something of the same sensibility might have made its way into
gelatin silver print or acrylic paint. The Whitney every two years
assembles a biennial exhibition meant to welcome the emerging
trends in American art, and any shift of aesthetic mood or intention was likely to show up on one or another of the walls at

Madison Avenue and East 75th Street. The exhibition filled the
museum's five floors with the work of eighty-two artists, most of
them in their thirties and many of them from California, but by
the time I had passed through six or seven galleries, I knew that
I was doomed to look at slogans and listen to speeches.

The button that served as proof of paid admission was stamped
with the message "I can't imagine ever wanting to be white," and
the preamble posted on the wall adjacent to the preferred point
of entry on the fourth floor spoke of "critical issues and important
questions," of "the function of art as socio-political critique," of
"the boundaries between art and pornography." The didactic tone
of voice reverberated through the whole of the exhibition like the
scolding of an angry governess, and even before I reached *Fist of
Light* or *Jack F; Forced to Eat His Own Excrement*, I understood that
the curators of the nation's conscience had compiled a syllabus of
moral attitudes deemed worthy of patient study and dutiful admiration. The attitudes took the form of art objects—composi-
tions in mixed and electronic media as well as sculpture and
painting—but they could as easily have been made manifest as
political leaflets or religious tracts. Most of the objects required a
close reading of the footnotes posted on a nearby wall. It was not
enough to merely look at the battered rubber woman or the home
movies of homosexual coupling, or the gold-plated tennis sneakers. It was also important to know that the artist "had come to
think about history as a dysfunctional idea" or that "these are the
people I live with; these are my friends; these are my family; this
is my self." The words that recurred in the wall notes—"identity,"
"imperialism," "difference," "otherness," "void," "oppression"—

were borrowed from the dictionary of academic literary criticism, and they all pointed as garishly as road signs to the injustices of gender, race, wealth, and social class. By the time I came across *Lard Gnaw* (a shambles of chewed lard mounted on a marble base), I knew that I was expected to read all the homework assignments and refrain from talking in class. The catalogue identified the lard as a "performative gesture" intended as a commentary on the "patriarchal community" that forces women into the "candy boxes" of "consumer fetishism."

None of the lectures in progress everywhere in the museum could be said to flatter or embrace all the assembled grievances, but an untitled fourth-floor installation made mostly of branding irons offered a fairly complete summary of the ruling sentiment. The installation occupied an entire room, and at first sight it was incomprehensible. Arranged in two long and ominous rows, the branding irons dangled from the ceiling in the center of the room, suggesting some sort of fence or jail, and the walls were decorated with what looked like a series of abstract drawings. The effect was both ugly and meaningless until I read the instructions and discovered that each of the branding irons had been forged in the typeface of Gregg shorthand. The two artists, both of them women educated at Brown University, had burned the stenographic symbols onto sheets of muslin, and it was these sheets, mounted on homosote and hung in bed frames, that were to be seen on the walls. Translated into English, the symbols formed single words ("kissing," "licking," "drugs," "intercourse") meant to be read as a communiqué from the frontiers of sexual violence.

After deciphering the riddle of the branding irons, I looked briefly at a collection of pornographic cartoons, read a few more wall messages (about "the psycho-technological mapping of the body" and "the neglected history of lesbian cinema"), and withdrew to the café on the ground floor of the museum to consider the text of the afternoon's lesson. At another table I heard a sophisticated blonde woman in a fur coat tell two German tourists that American magazines and newspapers employ the wrong kind of people to write art criticism. Always, she said, the editors think they owe a debt to a dead muse, and so they send people who have read Goethe and know where to look for Dresden on a map. "An awful mistake," she said. "They should send quacks. Art criticism is like movie criticism—a business for charlatans and frauds. Who else could bear to look at the pictures or read the catalogue?" By some accident of nature, she apparently had escaped the humiliations of branding irons and candy boxes, and the more somber of the two Germans took careful notes, interrupting her antic remarks to ask, please, for the meaning of "elitist crapola."

I take it for granted that most American art, like the bulk of American literature, aspires to the condition of a sermon or a social-science seminar, and so I didn't quarrel with the humorlessness of the exhibition. People dependent on foundation grants and government arts subsidies cannot afford to make jokes. Their talent is the talent for writing funding proposals, and their patrons demand high seriousness and statements of solemn purpose. They illustrate theories of moral and political reform, and they are as suspicious as college deans of unauthorized expressions of sensual or intellectual pleasure. Love is subversive and so is beauty, and joy is a word in Italian. Nor did I expect the exhibition to offer many hints or proofs of genius. In a commercial society people blessed with the gifts of the artistic imagination prefer to work for money, and I had seen all the techniques present on the four floors of the museum deployed to more dramatic effect as fashion design, as MTV film collage, as television advertisement, as Guns 'n' Roses concerts.

What was surprising about the exhibition was its oddly provincial character, as if it had been brought to New York by a committee of very earnest assistant professors amazed by the discovery that politicians sometimes tell lies. The rows of books displayed on the fourth floor (recommended reading for any bourgeois philistines who happened to be passing by) were the kind of texts apt to be seen in a window of a university bookstore during Women's Literature Week or Black History Month. The artists were young, but the doctrine was old. Wandering among the acrylic and the video screens, I noticed so many political tropes on loan from the attic of the late 1950s—the dehumanization of art, the individual lost in the lonely crowd, the imperial white man carried to and fro across the equator on the backs of noble black men, women in tears and the soul in chains—that I wondered where everybody had been for thirty years. Had anybody ever seen anything of the world except its representation in an art gallery in Cincinnati or Omaha? The canon of racial and sexual diversity was the stuff of department-store show windows and prime-time television, and over the same weekend that the Whitney opened its exhibition, the Clinton Administration indicated its intention to appoint several hundred new judges—many of them women or minorities—to the federal courts. To the artists making statements on the walls of the Whitney Museum, the news presumably was no more or less interesting than the news from medieval France or ancient Egypt.

As a course of political indoctrination, the biennial exhibition was not only well behind the times but also scornful of the uses of persuasion. If the artists meant to enlighten the audience, why then did they shout so many insults? To whom did they think they were addressing their remarks, and what dream of heaven did they have in mind? The reading room on the fourth floor provided a guest book in which patrons of the exhibition could express their opinions of what they had seen, and on the day that I saw the exhibition, the reviews were mostly bad:

> "The wasted energy on the first floor is an eco-crime."
> "Baudelaire had a phrase for mediocre artists—Les enfants gatés, spoiled children."
> "GWM—35—blond/blue eyes—looking for a sincere relationship."
> "So this is what happens to all the grad students who manage to get through college without learning how to paint."

Favorable reviews were few and brief, but toward the end of the guest book, neatly centered on the page in a handwriting that I took to be that of a professor accustomed to grading exams, I found a rebuttal that defied the mocking critics and set forth the premise of the exhibition:

"Ninety-nine percent of this audience needs this exhibit. Good going."

Here at last, possibly, was the point. The company of the spiritually elect had arrived from the innocent wilderness (at College Park, Maryland, or under the elm trees at Brown University) to denounce the wickedness of Sodom. It didn't matter that their art was hideous or their polemic as threadbare as the upholstery in a junkyard car. Ugliness was a proof of virtue, and so was the lack of talent. What was important was the scream of righteous fury. I doubt that many of the artists in the exhibition could have said what it was that they were angry about, but clearly something was very wrong with a world that didn't know their names, and maybe if they made some truly offensive "performative gesture," then Senator Jesse Helms might declare them enemies of the state and so rescue them from the pit of anonymity. The dream of heaven was a house in Bel-Air and a gospel of Hallmark cards as simple as the metaphysics of *Dances with Wolves*. Had they been asked to fill out a form indicating their theory of good and evil, I suspect that they would have reached a consensus along the following lines:

| *Good* | *Evil* |
|---|---|
| The self | The world |
| Feeling | Thought |
| Simplicity | Complexity |
| Equality | Liberty |
| Expression | Art |

| | |
|---|---|
| Adolescence | Maturity |
| Nature | Machinery |
| Innocence | Experience |
| The country | The city |

If only a very rich society can afford to sponsor so naive an aesthetic, only a still-puritan society confuses art with home- and self-improvement. By the end of the century maybe we will learn to do away with institutions as repressive as galleries and museums. Maybe the national endowments will simply let performance artists loose in the streets with pots of red paint, commissioning them to daub scarlet letters (S for Sexist, R for Racist, H for Heterosexual) on the foreheads of citizens suspected of harboring impure thoughts and incorrect opinions.

*May 1993*

# Performance Art

Nothing is so poor and melancholy as an art that is interested in
itself and not in its subject.
—GEORGE SANTAYANA

*I*t is never easy to ride a dead horse, but New York Mayor
Rudolph Giuliani managed to do so in late September when
he ordered the Brooklyn Museum of Art to withdraw an exhibition scheduled to open on October 2 or say goodbye to the
city's annual subsidy of $7.2 million. The mayor delivered the
ultimatum at a routine briefing for the City Hall press corps on
an otherwise dull Wednesday morning, and his tone was that of
a man surprised by yet another tax-exempt proof of human depravity. Surprised and mortally offended as a Catholic and a gentleman. No, he hadn't seen the exhibit assembled under the title
"Sensation: Young British Artists from the Saatchi Collection,"
but the illustrations in the museum catalogue suggested that it
was composed of some pretty "sick stuff"—a dead shark suspended
in a tank of formaldehyde, a sculpture carved in eight pints of
the sculptor's frozen blood, a biogenetic merger of fiberglass

schoolgirls tricked up with a penis where one would expect to find a nose, the artificial head of a cow decorated with a swarm of live maggots giving birth to flies. Even worse and most appallingly, the mayor had come across an image of the Madonna in which her right breast was indicated by a tiny clump of dried elephant dung.

"People are throwing elephant dung at a picture of the Virgin Mary," he said. "We will do everything that we can to remove funding from the Brooklyn Museum until the director comes to his senses."

The announcement set in motion another round of skirmishing in what have come to be known as "the culture wars," and over the course of the next three weeks the forces of light and darkness loosed a barrage of heavy rhetoric into the trenches of the news media. The museum filed a lawsuit under the flag of the First Amendment, the action undertaken "in the interests of all public institutions—museums, universities, and libraries—that are dedicated to the free exchange of ideas and information." Cadres of alarmed citizens associated the mayor with Stalinist Russia and Nazi Germany, rearming themselves with the catchphrases they had stockpiled during previous campaigns against government attempts to withhold public money from Robert Mapplethorpe's sexually explicit photographs, Andres Serrano's crucifix in a glass of his own urine, Karen Finley's smearing herself with chocolate. Notable literary figures, among them Norman Mailer, signed a full-page statement in the *New York Times* endorsing the principle of artistic freedom; eminent critics certified the virtues of elephant dung, its warmth, fertility, and earthbound symbolism; an ailing

John Cardinal O'Connor appeared in St. Patrick's Cathedral to say, in his Sunday homily, that he was saddened by the attack on "our blessed Mother."

I didn't read all the stories or follow all the turns of event, but by the time the exhibition opened to record crowds in Brooklyn, the several parties to the dispute had presented—collectively and unintentionally—a persuasive case for restructuring the government subsidies for the arts. No matter how rich or high-minded, a middle-class democracy fails in its efforts to bestow the gift of artistic patronage, and we might do ourselves a favor if we gave up the attempt to pretend otherwise.

The making of art in any of its more substantial forms (i.e., in forms likely to retain their energy and force over long periods of time) is an undemocratic occupation. The enterprise presupposes an individual acting without the advice or consent of a committee, also an audience, almost always small, that can afford to trust its own taste, prejudice, and judgment. Frederick the Great was enough of a musician to compose concerti for the flute and set old Bach a theme for a ricercar in three parts; the Elizabethan noblemen who funded Shakespeare could themselves write sonnets; the wives and daughters of the Hapsburg Court in eighteenth-century Vienna could play the music of Haydn and Mozart.

In a democratic republic the disbursement of government money to the arts devolves upon a body of earnest citizens (congressional committees, boards of well-meaning trustees, wealthy corporate sponsors) who construe their obligation as philanthropic, more fun to talk about than cancer or heart disease, as uplifting in its purpose as the ASPCA. Apt to be the kind of people who conceive of art as something made by children and sold to women through the medium of homosexuals, they find themselves in the business of doing good works, arranging courses in sensitivity training, building concert halls in vacant lots, throwing coins to beggars. Even assuming that they possessed an aesthetic of their own, they could not afford the luxury of indulging it. They bear a responsibility to the taxpayers or the stockholders, to the appearance of racial harmony, to the preferences of the chairman's wife and the claims of destitute school districts. The national genius for money and tables of organization domesticates the sometimes sinister waywardness of art into sunny moral lessons, and when confronted with an object about which somebody might have doubts, the pillars of the community (i.e., "the people who count," who sit on the committees and the boards of trustees) ask themselves whether they would let their eight-year-old daughters see it.

The elected or appointed Maecenas learns to think not of art but of a line of goods known as "The Arts." Art remains too much within the province of unreliable individuals not easily transposed into bureaucratic acronym. "The Arts" comprise any and all activity believed to be "creative." So defined and understood, they lend themselves to almost as many uses as religion—as a specific against crime, boredom, and drug addiction; as a palliative to send to slums, hospitals, and depressed coal-mining towns; as any hobby, craft, or innocent amusement that keeps people off the streets.

Mayor Giuliani pressed them into service as political statement, picking a quarrel with a museum to advertise his Senate election campaign and curry favor with those voters who might wish to see him as a champion of the old moral order, a defender of the Catholic faith, a friend of family values, the hope of innocence regained. His seeming to have been surprised by the discovery of foul and outrageous blasphemy in Brooklyn was as contrived as his presentation of himself as the Republican analogue of the shark floating in formaldehyde. His cultural advisers had known about the contents of the Brooklyn exhibition for at least nine months (had seen the slides, looked through the catalogue, reviewed the funding); familiar with the exhibition's promise to "investigate our culture's most pressing problems and persistent obsessions: class, race, and gender; normalcy and eccentricity; violence, disease, and death," they understood that what passes for modern art these days (a.k.a. "the cutting edge") often entails the sending of angry messages in blood-stained rope and broken glass, and they knew that Giuliani constructed his role as mayor on more or less the same set of artistic guidelines. At several meetings in which the mayor also had been present, nobody had raised any objections to the Brooklyn exhibition, and on the morning of September 22 the mayor's staff set up his tirade with a prepared question handed to an obliging reporter.

"Anything that I can do isn't art," the mayor said. "If I can do it, it's not art, because I'm not much of an artist. And I could figure out how to put this together. You know, if you want to throw dung at something, I could figure out how to do that."

The mayor was being far too modest. As accomplished a

thrower of dung as the late Jackson Pollock was a thrower of paint, the mayor has distinguished himself over the last six years by throwing it at jaywalkers and hot dog vendors, at the audience that listens to his weekly radio program, at anybody who doubts his virtue or questions his wisdom, at drunken drivers, gay activists, and the owners of striptease clubs, at the stray and overly ambitious squeegee man. When Hillary Clinton ventured to say that "our feelings of being offended should not lead to the penalizing and shutting down of an entire museum," Mayor Giuliani, as quick as ever with his move to the dung, smeared her with a malicious libel: "She agrees with using public funds to attack and bash the Catholic religion."

Like the mayor of New York, Arnold Lehman, the director of the Brooklyn Museum, also had a reason to misrepresent the nature of the art in the exhibition. What Lehman had on hand was a collection of stale avant-garde aesthetic theory, much of it dating from the 1950s, reworked in formaldehyde, updated with live maggots, annotated in elephant dung—i.e., the late-twentieth-century equivalent of nineteenth-century academic salon painting. Assembled by an advertising tycoon and billed as a tourist attraction, the exhibition had drawn gratifying numbers of people to the Royal Academy of Arts in London in the fall of 1997, and Lehman had acquired it as a ready-made success, in much the same way (and for most of the same reasons) that a theater manager in Detroit might have acquired the rights for a road-show production of a musical by Andrew Lloyd Webber. But the Americans were accustomed to the provocations of Howard Stern and Jerry Springer, and so Lehman thought it prudent to amplify the sound of the advance publicity. The museum commissioned David Bowie to narrate the audio tour and printed posters in the style of the "Health Warnings" on tobacco products—"The contents of this exhibition may cause shock, vomiting, confusion, panic, euphoria and anxiety. If you suffer from high blood pressure, nervous disorder or palpitations, you should consult your doctor."

So little was at risk, the art in question so safe and irrelevant, that the museum, like the mayor, turned it into advertising copy. The gift shop offered shark throw pillows, also souvenir clumps of elephant dung coated with hard gypsum to give them "a smooth, handsome appearance and an earthy appeal."

Lehman's dedication to the principles of commerce proved his worth as a loyal agent of the public-arts subsidy, somebody who could be trusted to do nothing dangerous, nothing that hadn't been done before (not once but many, many times), nothing likely to get anybody in trouble with a reckless display of an unfunded imagination—exactly the sort of man to whom a board of museum trustees could look for the best professional advice that money can buy and who could be relied upon to match this year's revolutionary sensation with last year's received wisdom, to polish the old Greek marble, or, as was required in Brooklyn, to restock an artificial cow's head with a weekly supplement of 20,000 fresh maggots.

Despite the proclamations of artistic freedom distributed to the newspapers, the prominent cultural institutions in New York were slow to protest the mayor's abridgment of the inalienable right to public money. Five days passed before anybody said anything, and when the expected letter finally arrived (deploring the "dangerous precedent" and "chilling effect" implicit in the mayor's vindictiveness) ten of the thirty-three members of the city's Cultural Institutions Group, among them Carnegie Hall and the New York State Theater, chose not to sign a document that might be interpreted as a waiver of their claim on next year's budget appropriation. The Metropolitan Museum of Art subscribed to the sentiment expressed in the letter, and its director, Philippe de Montebello, took the trouble to publish a clarification on the op-ed page of the *New York Times*. Yes, he had seen the Brooklyn exhibition, and it was, sad to say, very, very bad. He didn't disagree with the mayor's critical assessment, only with his perhaps too hasty impulse to censor and suppress. As a museum director himself, Montebello defended to the death a museum director's right to exhibit junk. Museum directors sometimes made mistakes, but eventually their crimes against conscience and taste came to judgment at the bar of eternity. "The suffrage of public opinion will ultimately have its say, but not before too many unwary visitors come to pay obeisance to art they feel they should try to understand and, Heaven forbid, even like."

The aesthetic response to the exhibition was the least of anybody's concerns. What was at issue were the political and commercial readings of the texts, and by the third week in October all the parties to the dispute were reporting tactical victories in their own sectors of the Culture War. The mayor had been proclaimed a hero by the kind of people who attribute the ruin of the country's moral principles to the pretentious New York art critics ("barbarians," the mayor said, who "put excrement on walls"); among people who believe that the United States is fast becoming a police state, the museum stood revealed as a stronghold of freedom, comforted in its distress by the friends of liberty and conscience while at the same time extracting campaign contributions (in the form of admission fees and gift-shop receipts) from the crowds showing up in record numbers to see the cow's head, the defiled Virgin, and the shark. If the museum for the time being had suffered the loss of its monthly allowance—the check for $497,554 failing to arrive on October 4—the odds favored its eventual return at the instruction of the City Council or a judge. The mayor's shows of outrage, coated with hypocrisy to give them "a smooth, handsome appearance and an earthy appeal," seldom lead to anything other than a headline. On no fewer than twenty-one occasions during his term in office he has moved to cancel the First Amendment rights of people whom he deems unsightly (jaywalkers, striptease dancers, gay and black activists, squeegee men, etc.), but he rarely wins the case in court. Playing to the television cameras, he stages effects as violent as those on exhibit in Brooklyn, safe in the knowledge that they will have been forgotten by the time they have been proved unconstitutional or worthless.

But in the meantime we have a successful work of postmodern performance art charged to the public expense, and if we can interpret the mayor's salary and maintenance costs as a cultural subsidy—similar to a grant given by the NEA to a music festival or an experimental-theater group—maybe we could settle the argument about the campaign finance laws. Never again would a politician be forced to depend upon the wickedness of corporate bribes. Let the candidates stand before the public as pictures in an exhibition, suspended in formaldehyde or giving birth to flies, and the voting public might pay to hear their stories told by David Bowie.

*December 1999*

# Potomac Fever

What grimaces, what capers, leaps and chuckles prime ministers,
presidents and kings must indulge in, in the privacy of their
bedrooms, so as to avenge their systems on the daylong strain
imposed on them!
—PAUL VALÉRY

With the onset of the presidential campaigning season,
Nicolson falls victim to one of the common delusions
of his trade. On most days of most seasons Nicolson
goes dutifully about the task of writing newspaper editorials
meant to keep the country safe from communists and fleas. But
in the autumn of every fourth year, when the weather turns cold
and the public opinion polls move their rigs north into New
Hampshire, Nicolson imagines that he was born to be a statesman
instead of a journalist.

Most journalists worthy of their rank suffer low-grade and
chronic symptoms of the same pathology, but in Nicolson the
affliction takes a peculiarly virulent form. During the worst of his
seizures he believes he would enjoy being President of the United
States. His hands sweat and he thinks he hears the cheering of

crowds. He broods about the ingratitude of a society that places so much of its trust and so many of its helicopters at the disposal of dolts. His humor turns choleric and he wonders why nobody asks him to make commencement speeches.

Fortunately for his wife and children (who otherwise might be condemned to a sequence of forced marches through the nation's shopping malls), Nicolson has the wit to know that unless he takes severe measures he would end like one of those garrulous derelicts sometimes seen explaining their geopolitical theories to ash cans in the park. Several years ago he devised a list of questions intended to restore his sense of democratic proportion. He presents the list to obliging friends with the instruction that they conduct the interrogation in a matter-of-fact voice appropriate to the reading of a catechism or police report.

When Nicolson showed up in the office the other day it was obvious that he had not been having an easy autumn. A tall and stoop-shouldered man, who once walked from Panama to Mexico City, he seemed drawn and pale, his eyes clouded by a distant stare. He pushed the familiar typescript across the desk and then, without saying a word, settled himself uncomfortably in a chair. After taking a few moments to light his cigarette, he indicated with a laconic nodding of his head that he was ready to answer questions. I began, as always, at the top of page one.

*What is it that presidents do?*

They keep up appearances and wear the iron masks of power. They tell the necessary lies with which other, more high-minded men would rather not incriminate themselves.

*What is the condition of a president's existence?*

Fragmented and incoherent. Somebody is always tugging at his sleeve, trying his patience, and nibbling at his time. He's lucky if he can remember his name, much less the capital of France.

*With whom do presidents consort?*

Mostly with the kind of people that decent citizens choose to avoid—with flatterers, office seekers, crooked lawyers, assassins, touts, arms merchants.

*Do presidents understand the workings of modern science?*
No.

*Of weapons and languages?*
No.

*Of art or culture?*
No.

*Do presidents possess extraordinary gifts of wisdom or perception?*

On the contrary, their ignorance is their strength. If they knew what they were doing they would find it impossible to act.

*How would you describe a presidential election?*
An ordeal by klieg light.

*How does the electorate reach its judgment?*
On the basis of the single slogan or facial expression that the

audience can be counted upon to remember for more than fifteen minutes, because of the color of the candidate's tie or the nervousness of his hands.

*Name the attributes of a winning candidate.*

Stamina, courage, energy, and a strong stomach. The candidate must travel thousands of miles, bear the insults of ill-informed experts, eat the food in Holiday Inns, submit to the charade of a debate, answer (in twenty words or less) questions that cannot be answered in 100,000 words, display under all circumstances and any weather not the least sign of fear or disgust.

*What is the cost of a president's ambition?*

Ruinous and of two kinds. First, the cost to the nation. Presidents must be seen doing great deeds, and these inevitably require huge sums of money. The waste is as colossal as the president's appetite for praise.

Second, the heavy tax on the lives of the people in the president's immediate vicinity. The governor of even a small New England state marks the passage of his career with an emotional desolation as bleak as the wreckage behind the caravans of Genghis Khan. Look into the face of a candidate's wife, and you look into an abyss.

*List the attributes of a successful president.*

Selfishness and a cold egoism. A willingness to sacrifice other people's interests to one's own. Also a talent for dissimulation, a capacity to endure boredom and to turn one's back on the unlucky or unsuccessful. Better the man who can order the incineration of cities with a cozy smile than the man who worries about the death of whales.

*What is the president's reward for these crimes against conscience and humanity?*

Applause, the servility of all those who approach him, a lot of space in the papers, and a lot of time on television. Also the comfort implicit in a surrounding din of gossip, sirens, cheering, and noise.

*What does a president hope to achieve? Toward what vision of the future does he push his way through the crowd?*

He doesn't know. He moves instinctively deeper into the labyrinth of his megalomania, snuffling toward the scent of something more—more weapons, more friends, more secrets, more lies, more power.

*Why should we feel grateful for the services of men blessed with such a monstrous appetite and rare pathology?*

What other kind of men could bear the weight of our expectation?

At this point Nicolson's eyes had begun to clear. His expression seemed less furtive, his voice more confident and kind. There were a few additional questions on his list, but Nicolson indicated that the delusion had passed; for the time being, at least, he could follow the political news without feelings of envy or resentment.

Happy to be relieved of his burden, he picked up his text and went off to write what he referred to as "a pawky, God-fearing, patriotic sort of piece" for the Sunday edition.

*October 1984*

# *Hugo, Mon Amour*

Given the state of the art of prime-time television, I wouldn't be surprised if next season's hit dramatic series presented as its hero a brave and handsome suitcase. Obviously the suitcase would need to be expensive, from Vuitton, Gucci, or Mark Cross, and large enough to carry most of the toys and products synonymous with American success. Maybe it couldn't accommodate a Mercedes-Benz, but certainly it would be spacious enough for cashmere coats, silver flatware, digital stereos, Mont Blanc pens, silk scarves, top hats, delft tiles, and linzer tortes.

By casting a suitcase as the hero, the producers could do away with the increasingly tiresome and irrelevant business of portraying human character, feeling, and motive. All concerned could move directly to their passion for the objects ennobled by happy association with status and money.

The preoccupation with things is color-coordinated with the spirit of the age. The obsession shows up in the policies of the Reagan administration as well as in the photographs published by *Architectural Digest* and the short stories published by *The New*

*Yorker*. But, as with so much else, television can come more crassly to the point.

Reduced to their properly ceremonial roles as acolytes in the sanctuaries of wealth, the supporting actors could pack and unpack the suitcase while miming appropriate responses to the merchandise. The opportunities for dramatic expression encompass the entire arc of emotion of which prime-time television is capable, and the actors could choose among an inventory of attitudes and poses:

*Wild and reckless joy*—while packing the suitcase with a dress by Halston or a suit from Dunhill.

*Elegiac melancholy*—on unpacking Grandmother's set of Lowestoft china.

*Domestic happiness*—while folding a flannel nightgown or a child's school uniform.

*Disgust*—on being obliged to touch a plastic raincoat bought at Sears.

*Lasciviousness*—while fondling satin lingerie.

*Fear*—on finding a severed head among the new shirts from Turnbell and Asser.

*Humor*—while packing feather boas and old baseball mitts to be given away as prizes at a charity auction in Palm Springs.

*Tragic sorrow*—on discovering at the bottom of the suitcase a threadbare Chanel blouse bought twenty years ago in Cap d'Antibes when the world was young.

The telling of the suitcase's many heartwarming and poignant stories undoubtedly would require the art of Aaron Spelling. Perhaps the richest and most successful impresario of prime-time comparison shopping, Mr. Spelling already has introduced his audiences to the opulence of the goods and services displayed on *Dynasty*, *Fantasy Island*, *The Love Boat*, and *Hotel*.

Presumably the suitcase would have a name, and I think Hugo has the right sound. The name implies a reassuring degree of affluence and carries with it the faint air of passivity thought to be attractive among the children, as well as the possessions, of the rich. Nobody could mistake Hugo for a third-rate vinyl suitcase used to staying in motels on the outskirts of Mobile, Alabama. Hugo is a genuine-leather suitcase, a distinguished and self-assured suitcase accustomed to being carried through the lobbies of first-class hotels.

If Hugo could speak, he would sound a lot like Gerald Ford or Blake Carrington. The audience instinctively would know this because Hugo resembles Gerald Ford and Blake Carrington in stature and manner. Things just sort of happen to Hugo, in the same way they just sort of happen to Gerald Ford and Blake Carrington, and Hugo responds with the same intensity of expression.

Fortunately, it isn't necessary for Hugo to speak. Hugo's silence is more eloquent than words. The mere sight of Hugo is enough to convey the state of Hugo's feeling. If Hugo is seen being reverently packed with jewels and caviar and silk, then the audience knows that all is well. Conversely, if Hugo is seen being loaded down with broken cameras and dirty sneakers (i.e., as if his

condition in life were no different from that of a common shopping bag), the audience knows that Hugo is in trouble.

Spelling's scriptwriters have been assigned more preposterous
tasks, and they shouldn't have much trouble devising plotlines
that entangle Hugo in the romance of the world. I can imagine
Hugo rescued from a sunken yacht, Hugo sold at Sotheby's, Hugo
in a plane wreck, Hugo in the hands of the KGB, Hugo submit-
ting to the indignity of a search by Turkish customs agents, Hugo
abducted by fur thieves, Hugo placed with the servants' luggage
during a weekend house party in East Hampton or Monte Carlo.

Nor would it be impossible to involve Hugo in the kind of
transient love affairs that distract or amuse the protagonists of
police and detective dramas. Like the champions of liberty who
wander around Los Angeles in search of new adventure, Hugo
never has time to stay. The camera could see him reclining briefly
but meaningfully behind a concierge's desk with a sexy little overnight bag; in other episodes Hugo could be trapped in an elevator
at the Ritz-Carlton with a sable coat, or spend the night with a
matched pair of Samsonite cases in the luggage bay of a 747 en
route to Japan.

The casting of a suitcase as hero offers a number of further
advantages to the owners of the show. A suitcase is always a contented and thoroughly professional member of the creative team.
Unlike Joan Collins, a suitcase has little use for hairdressers or
chauffeured limousines. Also, it is easier to arrange personal appearances for a suitcase, not only in shopping malls and on the
Carson show but also in cameo roles in Spelling's other entertain-

ments—Hugo rowed ashore to *Fantasy Island*, Hugo lost in the lobby of *Hotel*, Hugo rolled up the gangplank of *The Love Boat*.

Were Hugo to become a star, then, at about the same time he appeared on the cover of *TV Guide*, Spelling's business people could begin to charge usurious fees to the merchants who wish Hugo to be seen carrying their products to San Francisco or Zanzibar. Let the show run for three or four years, and Hugo's endorsement might elect a president.

*January 1986*

# Tremendous Trifles

I have often observed that nothing ever perplexes an adversary
so much as an appeal to his honor.
—BENJAMIN DISRAELI

Senator Bill Bradley showed up in Greenwich Village in
early June to parade his virtues as a presidential candidate
before an audience of about 500 people at New School University, and halfway through the program it occurred to me that
if Thorstein Veblen were still sitting in the hall, he would have
regarded the senator as the political equivalent of a marble birdbath or a pet pony. Veblen joined the faculty of the New School
in the 1920s, some years after he published *The Theory of the Leisure
Class*, and Bradley presented a brilliant proof of the hypothesis for
which Veblen coined the term "conspicuous consumption," or, in
his more sardonic paragraphs, "honorific waste."

An economist by profession and by inclination a satirist, Veblen
derived his theory from the study of the upper ranks of American
society at the zenith of the Gilded Age. The idle gentry then in
residence in New York City and Newport, Rhode Island, were in

the habit of spending extravagant sums of money on oysters and ball gowns (also on parrots, top hats, gold-headed walking sticks, and croquet tournaments), and Veblen suggested that the ferocious consumption of an always more elaborate store of superfluous goods testified to their "pecuniary decency" and thus to their inward states of grace. The man who could afford to fill a fishpond with champagne was a man in close and constant touch with Providence.

Senator Bradley quite clearly met the definition of a superfluous good, his campaign money provided by our own modern reincarnations of Veblen's late-nineteenth-century railroad and banking tycoons (i.e., by Robert Redford, David Geffen, Michael Eisner, Dustin Hoffman, Michael Jordan, etc.) and his presence (in a room or on a ballot) demonstrating little else except the moral refinement of his patrons. Seated on the stage with the editor of *Parade* magazine—a servile gentleman who asked questions in the manner of a butler presenting grapes or buttered toast—the senator began by telling the story of his birth on the banks of the Mississippi River, his idyllic childhood under the sycamore trees in a small town true to the memory of Tom Sawyer and Huckleberry Finn, his going to Princeton and Oxford University, afterward to the N.B.A. with the New York Knicks, and so to Washington, a latter-day Mr. Smith, proud to serve his country as a senator from New Jersey. Not that he ever did or said anything that anybody could remember, but the modest telling of so sunny a success story (in a voice both reasonable and barely audible) set up the good news of the senator's Great Awakening. During his travels with the basketball team, and then again during his years in Congress, he came to know and love the American people, went out to meet them, listened to what they had to say, knew that he was on the right track when he and a citizen with whom he was enjoying an emotional encounter embraced each other in a flood of warm and honest tears.

Asked by the editor of *Parade* to define a "meaningful life," the senator mentioned the need to "engage another human being at a deep, personal level." His listening to black people taught him important lessons about the racial prejudice that still disfigured the America not pictured in the beer commercials. When his wife was stricken with breast cancer, he learned that every day is precious, also to "seize the moment," "lead from your convictions," "speak fully from your heart."

And why was he running for president? Because he knew he could provide the "leadership" that has been missing from all our lives. And what did he stand for? For life, liberty, and the pursuit of happiness. And how did he propose to mend the American political system that he had declared irreparably broken when he retired from the Senate in 1996? Campaign finance reform, calling the media to the higher altitudes of conscience. The entire content of the conversation (preserved on film for the Library of Congress, said the editor of *Parade*, for the benefit of "men and women yet to be born") could have been reduced to a message printed on a box of Wheaties.

But so also could the campaign messages being delivered elsewhere in the country by Hillary Clinton, George W. Bush, and Steve Forbes. Because none of them possesses the specific knowledge or experience likely to fit them for the offices they seek, they present themselves as edifying models of conduct and deportment, remarkable for their delicacy of feeling, their "compassionate conservatism," and their deep concern for orphaned children and Cape Sable seaside sparrows. All the candidates endorse the cause of civility and recommend a show of sympathy for the suffering of one's fellow man. Bradley told his audience at the New School that when listening to particularly sad stories, he often said to himself, There but for the grace of God go I.

A month earlier, speaking to a reporter for the *New York Times* about her Senate campaign, Mrs. Clinton had said, "I think it would be a very good thing, not only for Buffalo or Erie County or New York but our whole country, for each of us to take a deep breath and think, you know, There but for the grace of God go I." Steve Forbes, meanwhile, in a television commercial commissioned from the advertising agency famous for its repositioning of Mrs. Paul's Fish Sticks, echoed Bradley's theme about the goodness of the American people. Seated in a high-ceilinged room distinguished by a gathering of important drapes, an effect suggestive not only of the White House but also of the Vanderbilt mansion in Newport employed as the set for Robert Redford's *Great Gatsby*, Forbes said that he stood foursquare for "truly realizing the American dream, which, as you know, is allowing each of us and all of us the chance to discover and develop to the fullest our God-given talents."

Veblen might not have recognized the set decorations or the background music, but the passage of a hundred years hasn't dimmed the force of his observations about the character of a society in which the aptitude for acquisition stands as the definitive measure of self-esteem. As the nation has prospered, the leisure class has increased and multiplied, assimilating lower social orders formerly regarded as subservient or ancillary (Hollywood movie stars and Harvard professors, as well as expensive divorce lawyers and Washington television journalists) and enlarging the sphere of its amusements.

The habits of spending favored at the turn of the twentieth century by the privileged few now characterize the society as a whole, and what was once the leisure class has become the leisure state. Devoted to the displays of honorific waste, the government at Washington employs an opulent household of domestic servants (upper, lower, congressional, regulatory, etc.) comprising as many as three million clerks, functionaries, orators, consultants, briefing officers, press and appointment secretaries, aides de camp, weapons analysts, chauffeurs, grooms, speechwriters, cooks, media spokespersons, and teachers of aerobics. A staff undreamed of in the philosophy of Alva Vanderbilt or August Belmont, performing what Veblen would have recognized as the tasks of vicarious leisure. They consume the master's goods as proof of the master's ability to pay for their superfluity; the less that is required of them, the more eloquently they testify to their master's wealth and prowess.

The bulk of the money available to the country's political campaigns comes from the relatively small cadre of high-end sponsors (a list of maybe 200,000 names, some of them individuals, most of them corporations, trade associations, and special-interest groups) who write the checks for sums in excess of $1,000. Our democracy now consists of this one constituency (known to Veblen in 1899 as "the radiant body" of American wealth and wisdom), which reserves to itself the right to choose the candidates, hire the bands, blow up the balloons.

Even in Veblen's day, ostensibly purposeless leisure had begun to lose its value as an "unremitting demonstration of ability to pay." The man who wished to make a successful appearance at a golf club or class reunion couldn't simply say that he had been sitting in a chair for eight months. The canon of reputable leisure obliged him to speak with some degree of knowledge about antique furniture or the breeding of greyhounds. The more useless the occupation in question, the more credit accrued to his account. A knowledge of medieval Latin commanded more respect than a knowledge of contemporary Italian. The modern forms of etiquette require earnest professions of faith in a democracy now almost entirely ceremonial.

The immense prosperity of the last twenty years has admitted so many new members to the precincts of the leisure class that the competition for a place in the important gossip columns (i.e., the ones devoted to national political affairs) has become a good deal more severe. In the late 1890s a man could acquire a reputation for gravitas by squandering a fortune on polo mallets; in the late 1990s so many people can do likewise that the expenditure no longer satisfies the criteria of honorific waste. But not everybody can afford to bankroll a presidential campaign as hopeless as Bill Bradley's or pay the prices demanded by Bill and Hillary Clinton for an evening in the Lincoln Bedroom, and the man who can say that he has been traveling in China with Al Gore and a Buddhist nun attains a higher rung of status than the man who has been going to trade fairs or drifting around the Caribbean on a cruise ship. Discussions nominally political thus become questions of aesthetics. Does Elizabeth Dole wear fur coats? Can Steve Forbes ride a horse? Is Al Gore really made of wood?

During the same week that I listened to Senator Bradley express the hope that once elected president he could nudge "our collective humanity a half-inch forward," I blundered into a quorum of journalists taking up the question of Hillary Clinton's wish to become a senator from New York. The three women present in the bar of the Algonquin Hotel complained of her effrontery and gall—"a brass-faced carpetbagger" whose increasingly frequent visits to the city made a mess of midtown traffic. They could see little else in her face except self-righteous certainty and devouring ambition (the same expression that they noticed in the face of Special Prosecutor Kenneth Starr), and they thought a candidate for the Senate should feel some sort of attachment to (or connection with) the state that he or she sought to represent.

The older of the two gentlemen in the company pointed out that Robert Kennedy was still a registered voter in Massachusetts when he was elected senator from New York in 1965 but that within a month of taking office he knew where to find both Mott Street and Coney Island. Hillary Clinton was a quick study, he said, and she wouldn't have much trouble remembering that the

Yankees play in the Bronx, the Knicks in Madison Square Garden, the Giants in New Jersey. Sigourney Weaver had played the wife of the American president in the movie *Dave* (played the part a good deal more convincingly than Mrs. Clinton was apt to play a New York senator), but nobody had asked her to conduct a tour of the White House or explain our foreign policy in the Balkans.

The younger gentleman, a writer for an online magazine and somewhat closer to the spirit of the times, didn't find anything wrong with carpetbagging. A standard American operating procedure, he said, endorsed by the managers of Wall Street hedge funds as well as by the owners of suburban shopping malls and the proprietors of major league baseball teams. Did anybody think that when George Steinbrenner chose his infielders he gave much thought to their affection for (or acquaintance with) their nominal hometown? Business school professors advised against the signing of loyalty contracts with any particular city or set of map coordinates, informing their students that the big money must be free to come and go as it pleases, all the deals in transit and all the employees migrant. Why deny to politicians the privileges extended to a junk bond?

What was interesting about the conversation was the absence of any reference to a topic in the news. Just as Senator Bradley on the stage of the New School had declined to spread the cloak of his noble intentions in the mud of a public and ambiguous event (no mention of the bombing of Yugoslavia or the shooting in Colorado's Columbine High School, nothing about the drug trade, abortion, Al Gore, welfare reform, or the cost of medical insurance), so also the journalists at the Algonquin didn't think it necessary to mention Mrs. Clinton's views on Israel or adultery. They were concerned with the questions of stylish performance, with the way words look and sound, not what they supposedly mean, and they could as easily have been talking about Sigourney Weaver.

I don't know why I should have been surprised. Twenty years ago in a New York bar, at least one of the journalists present would have inquired as to the whereabouts of "representative self-government," issued a statement on behalf of "we, the people," and remembered that the American promise granted poor citizens the same liberties enjoyed by the presidents of General Motors and Mobil Oil. These days the conversations dwell on the wonders of the Internet and the miracle of the stock market. The lack of interest in the purpose of a democratic politics corresponds to the steadily declining rate of attendance at the November voting booths. For the most part, I meet amused spectators (college students as well as newspaper columnists, also trial lawyers and history professors) content to look upon the presidential campaigns in much the same way that Veblen looked at the summer social season in Newport—as a never-ending round of dog shows and masquerade balls staged by a leisure class rich enough to afford the costumes, the hairdressers, and the time.

*August 1999*

# *Conventional Wisdom*

January 20, 2001

Yale University
Department of History
Professor Walter Trumbull
320 York Street
New Haven, Connecticut 06520

Dear Walter,

I never like to get in the way of your enthusiasms, and I have
no quarrel with your demand for a constitutional convention. You
write, as always, in the voice of the eighteenth century, and your
letters are a joy to read. I especially admired your reference to last
year's presidential campaign as "an enfeebled dithering of opinion
polls," both candidates "borne aloft on great billows of empty
oratory." With respect to the voting in Florida, I can't argue
with your disgust. As you say, a "travesty and an outrage," possibly also "a shameless theft"; in any event a poor lesson to set
before the nation's schoolchildren as well as our enemies abroad,

undoubtedly an encouragement to common pickpockets and apprentice tyrants.

You have a way with words, Walter, and I'm sure the country would profit from a government more responsive to the will of the people. I see no reason why we shouldn't begin again with cell phones in place of goose-quill pens—disband the Electoral College, bring the length of the primary campaigning season somewhat closer to the term of the trout season in Montana, augment the Bill of Rights, require the candidates for the Senate to pass some sort of civil-service examination, replace the office of the presidency with an Executive Council similar to the one proposed by Benjamin Franklin.

All good points, Walter, well and truly taken, but you say nothing about television and less about the valet parking. Nor do you take account of the product endorsements and the towel service. Little things, all of them tiresome and none of them as important as the question of states' rights, but they add up, the little things, and pretty soon, always when you least expect it, there they are, standing between you and the truth.

I know that you regard the television screen with loathing and contempt, but how else, or where else, do you "bestow upon the American people the long-deferred inheritance of their democratic birthright"? The Internet won't do it. Who would read, much less ratify, a Constitution composed by elflike nerds? The document requires approval by both houses of Congress and thirty-eight state legislatures, and the interested parties would think they were looking at a printout submitted by the Unabomber.

You will remember that Arianna Huffington staged what she

billed as "Shadow Conventions" last summer in both Philadelphia and Los Angeles; presumably you also will remember that they were seen as marginal entertainments. The major media didn't show up. Instead of Dan Rather and the editor of *Le Monde,* we had a collection of guitar players, three correspondents from *The Nation*, four friends of Ralph Nader, several delegates from the Seattle street protests (two of them dressed as endangered sea turtles), a lot of speeches (impassioned but familiar) about the mindless and uncaring greed of the New York banks. You would have endorsed every declaration of democratic principle, but if I read your letter correctly you have a more ambitious project in mind, "something serious and genuinely revolutionary," and for that kind of program we need a serious and genuinely revolutionary sum of money.

The managers of last year's presidential campaigns weren't attempting anything brilliant—just trying to get by as cheaply as possible with an old script, two candidates without much draw at the box office, three harmless debates, and a $750 million production budget well below the price of a second-rate record company or a losing football team. You're talking about a major motion picture—a thousand delegates, the convention in session for at least a year, inspirational rhetoric, a born-again America. I know that these are dark days in the life of the republic, Walter, and I don't disagree that dark days call for strong measures.

Not for a moment do I disparage your purpose or doubt your intent, but if what we have in mind is "a citizens' initiative," I don't think we can ask for federal money. Entirely the wrong impression, Walter. We mean to promote our delegates as the philosophical heirs and democratic assigns of Jefferson's independent yeoman, and we don't want to look like beggars dancing for government dimes. Even if we obtained a grant from the Library of Congress or the National Endowment for the Humanities, the level of funding wouldn't pay for the construction of Ted Koppel's skybox.

Nor can we appeal to one or more of the nonprofit organizations concerned with the questions of good government—Common Cause, The Pew Charitable Trusts, the American Enterprise Institute, etc., etc. We would find ourselves too easily identified with somebody else's political agenda. Take money from The Heritage Foundation, and the *New York Times* smears us with the mud of right-wing extremism; accept a contribution from the Sierra Club, and the *Wall Street Journal* consigns us to the scrap heap of the imbecile left.

Which—and I'm sure you don't want to hear me say this, Walter—brings us to the corporations. I know your feeling on the subject, I've heard you talk about the "fetid breath of corporate bagmen," but who else has the money? Who else bears the brand-name images of America's long abiding friends? Try to ignore— just for the moment and in the interest of the greater cause—the bad news in the small print about monopoly, price-fixing, "disappeared" middle management, outright fraud, assembly-line workers both maimed and dead. Reconstitute the form of government, and you'll have time enough to revisit the subtexts. But first things first, and for the time being we're discussing hotel suites, shuttle buses, registration desks, where to rent the chairs. The corporations spent $1.3 billion sponsoring last year's Olympic Games, and they worry about the continuing failure of the country's schools. Persuade Intel and IBM that a constitutional convention is a massive public-works project, like Hoover Dam or the building of the atom bomb, and then you can begin to think about delegates and possible topics of debate.

You say you want everybody present to know the difference between a property and a civil right, to come prepared to speak intelligently on issues both foreign and domestic, to refer with ease to *The Federalist* papers as well as to the collected works of Henry Adams. I take your point, Walter, but I think you set the bar a trifle high. It's conceivable that you could ask the prospective delegates to pass a short quiz (one page, twenty questions, true or false) touching on a few of the more prominent events in the nation's history (who won the Civil War, where Bunker Hill is, what happened to the Black-feet and the Crow), but how can you not make concessions to celebrity?

The network audience wants to see people who count for something in the world, people comparable in wealth and social rank to the original authors of the Constitution in Philadelphia in the summer of 1787. As you well know, Walter, they were gentlemen whose names preceded them with the glow of privilege and the weight of authority. I've read your monographs on Charles Pinckney and Gouverneur Morris, both of them figures equivalent in stature to our own Bill Gates, Oprah Winfrey, Ted Turner,

Martha Stewart. Why, then, do you choose to forget the country's roots in oligarchy?

Except for a C-SPAN audience in a Minneapolis bookstore, who wants to listen to debate on the topic of proportional representation? The question enlivened the conversation in 1787 because the eighteenth-century colonies were synonymous with specific concentrations of wealth—merchant shipping in the North, tobacco plantations in the South. But now that wealth has slipped its ties to place, why pretend otherwise? As you say, it no longer takes four days to go by coach from Boston to New York, and if you intend a new Constitution to reflect the twenty-first-century reality, why balk at acknowledging George Steinbrenner and Donald Trump as our own abridged editions of Roger Sherman and Rufus King?

Select the delegates by virtue of their approval ratings in *Forbes* or *Fortune* magazine, not for reasons having to do with the accidents of geography. If you wish to assemble a company of the elect, allot four places (two men, two women) to each of the country's 200 richest commercial interests (the banks, the news and entertainment media, grain and retail merchants, etc.) and the same number in the same proportion to the leading noncommercial enterprises (universities, hospitals, churches, charitable foundations, etc.). It doesn't matter whether everybody brings something to say. George Washington attended every session in Philadelphia, and not once in four months did he speak a single word to any point in any of the debates. The embodiment of gravitas, very dignified, a presence as reassuring as a marble bust of Cicero. You can depend upon performances equally impressive from both Charlton Heston and Justice Clarence Thomas.

You suggest putting the convention out to bid among the nation's historically important cities, possibly also to Las Vegas or Colonial Williamsburg. Again I take your point (venerable architecture, postcard monuments), but again I think that we'd be making a mistake. Remember that you're condemning 1,000 delegates to sit in meetings for the better part of a year. Leave them too long in any one city, and the convention takes on the character of a regional sales promotion. The television audience grows bored with the sight of overly familiar palm trees, the same batteries of revolutionary cannon, yet another cable car clanging toward the wonder of San Francisco Bay.

The eighteenth-century authors of the Constitution managed to get through the work in four months because they were keenly interested in politics, not easily distracted, accustomed to the habits of hard and sustained study. Not our kind of landed plutocracy, Walter. Our people don't like to read books, and their attention spans bear comparison to the life expectancies of moths. We'd begin to lose them in the strip clubs, and the next thing you know the convention becomes the butt of an evening's jokes on Letterman or Leno.

We're better off with a road show set up along the lines of a professional golf tour. The corporations understand the format, know and love the game, and the tournaments invariably bring with them the prospect of sudden fortune somewhere on a sunny fairway or a gently contoured green. Let the convention move its venue every week—under canvas at a fairground near St. Louis, to the civic auditorium in Wichita or the racetrack in Fort Worth—and it comes to town with the promise of a traveling circus. Technicians setting up hospitality tents and television towers, blimps drifting in the sky, limousines bearing the gifts of Hollywood celebrity. If we can impart to the convention something of the same excitement, we achieve an atmosphere of great good feeling and a sense of a work importantly in progress. Every week a new and heartwarming view of America the Beautiful—wonderful photographs of the Arizona desert, the Colorado mountains, the sea at Monterey—and none of the participants in town long enough to attract the notice of the tabloids or the police.

Given the drift and bias of the notes so far in hand, Walter, I'm beginning to suspect that a constitutional convention isn't as good an idea as it seemed when I first read your letter. I think I understand what you mean by a popular assembly, but I'm afraid that you have in mind a symposium attended by the faculty at Yale. That's not the crowd apt to be standing around with the big money on the first tee at Pebble Beach. Set up the procedure for designing a new and improved government, and we're likely to lose the few liberties we still retain. You're familiar with the moral jingoism of Robert Bork; you know that the country's major corporations routinely screen job applicants for impurities in their urine and their speech. Present such people with the chance to play the part of philosopher kings, and we can expect the right to stand for public office awarded only to those citizens whose incomes exceed $500,000 a year, and the residents of large cities reduced, as were the South's plantation slaves, to the measure of three fifths of a person and a vote.

Probably we should be glad that the gentlemen who wrote the Constitution were as suspicious of efficient government as they were wary of the "turbulence and folly" that they associated with the theory and practice of democracy. By containing the powers of government in a mechanism as finely balanced as a late-eighteenth-century ornamental clock, they distributed political energy among so many weights and counterweights that nobody could say for certain how the movement originated or where sovereignty was to be found. Why give the friends of John Ashcroft and the insurance companies a chance to correct the mistake? Resist the temptation to send a copy of the letter to *Newsweek,* and know that I remain, together with Benjamin Franklin,

Your Humble Servant
and Careful Friend

*March 2001*

# Hide-and-Go-Seek

A frivolous society can acquire dramatic significance only
through what its frivolity destroys.
—EDITH WHARTON

*E*dith Wharton was speaking of the light-minded company
seated on the velvet sofas of America's Gilded Age, but
the remark sums up the news from the nation's capital
since President Clinton lost, at least for the time being and until
the referees in Congress have had time to review the game films,
last summer's deciding round of hide-and-go-seek. Frivolity implies attempted escape from boredom, also surfeit, egoism, stupidity, and trivial amusement, and under one or another of those
headings it's possible to account for much of the nervous gossip,
most of the striking of indignant moral poses, nearly all of the
destruction.

Maybe if we lived in a country serious about its politics, protective of its freedoms, proud of its public institutions (i.e., the
America described in commencement speeches and pictured on
the postcards), President Clinton might have resigned last Janu-

ary, before the name and caricature of Monica Lewinsky tumbled
onto the stage of *Saturday Night Live*. If we possessed a government
by no means perfect but one that a useful number of people still
thought worth the trouble to honor and preserve, President Clinton could have resigned on August 17, the day he testified before
the grand jury and offered the network television audience the
first of his grudging concessions to the truth. By failing to resign
on September 6 or 7, soon enough to suppress the publication of
Kenneth Starr's foul-mouthed referral, the President, together
with the special prosecutor, served notice of his contempt—for
the office of the president of the United States, for what little
remains to the country of its trust in government, for anybody
fool enough to take him at his word.

The unctuous prayers and smirking news analysis that seeped
out of Washington over the weekend of September 12 suggest
that we don't live in a country protective of its freedoms or proud
of its public institutions. Maybe I draw too broad a conclusion,
make too much of what I read in the papers or see on television,
but I don't know how else Clinton could have been twice elected
president except by an audience hoping to relieve its boredom and
an electorate careless enough to construe its politics as a trivial
amusement or a schoolyard game.

By the time Clinton stood for his second term in the prosperous
autumn of 1996 the voters surely were well enough acquainted
with his character to know him as a man ruled by expedience,
probably a philanderer, certainly a liar. But he put up a good
show, talking the talk of a media discourse in which feeling out-
points thought, fluent in the sound-bite language made welcome

on *The Wonderful World of Disney,* where public debate becomes private therapy, the measures of achievement register as magnitudes of celebrity, and what was once a citizenry looks to Oprah or Larry King to dramatize the meaning of the Constitution.

When the price or time was right, Clinton told uplifting presidential parables about flood victims and school uniforms, and on slow news days, when nobody was bombing Atlanta or Oklahoma City, he supplied the warm gruel of Harlequin Romance. Somewhere offstage he was forever being followed by men in raincoats, and the looming of a supermarket scandal imbued his presidency with the excitement of an episode of *Law & Order.*

The 1996 campaign debate was mostly a matter of releasing balloons, its feeble motion seconded by the poor showing at the November polls. Only 49.08 percent of the eligible voters bothered to attend what they apparently had come to regard as an invitation to some sort of tiresome charity event. Among the even smaller minority that still took the trouble to follow the political news, opinion was largely shaped by the media loyal to the dogma of their corporate owners. The prevailing orthodoxy held that politics was a subsidiary function of economics and democracy an agreeable by-product of capitalism. The world's parliaments served at the pleasure of the world's markets; legislators came and went like fruit flies, but the money lived forever, which was why it didn't matter who occupied the White House. Elect a saxophone; send in a clown. With some decent luck and a little help from the men in the raincoats (chief among them Kenneth Starr), handsome Bill Clinton's second term in office might turn out to be as much fun as Rush Limbaugh or throwing pies.

The Republican majority in Congress delighted in the fiesta theme of politics as trivial pursuit. Nearly always good for an entertaining headline while at the same time filling legislative orders for its corporate patrons (the banking and telecommunications bills, the easing of the capital-gains tax, etc.), Congress deftly avoided the questions (about medical care, social security, education, campaign-finance reform, etc.) likely to arouse suspicion of a genuine political debate. Newt Gingrich, the Speaker of the House, shut down the machinery of the federal government for twenty-seven days in 1995 and early '96 because he wasn't received aboard Air Force One with the courtesy he deemed appropriate to his self-styled rank as "Teacher of the Rules of Civilization." His pretensions to moral grandeur fell apart like a trick chair with the discovery that his talent for money laundering matched, possibly even surpassed, his knowledge of Aristotle.

President Clinton meanwhile was so busy playing games of let's pretend with Paula Jones and Kenneth Starr that he didn't have time to do much of anything else. Brilliant in the performance of his ceremonial duties—handing out ballpoint pens in the White House Rose Garden, dismissing a surgeon general for her mention of the word "masturbation," apologizing for slavery, exhorting the nation's teenage youth to take the vow of chastity—somehow he never quite managed to cast the airiness of his rhetoric in anything other than Platonic forms. Nobody expected him to do otherwise.

A president suckled on the sound bites of the electronic media (salt-free, risk-averse, baby-soft), Clinton came of age in a society guided by talk-show hosts, captained by lawyers, inspired by actors, educated by press agents—all of them the kind of people paid to arrange and rearrange the truth in its most flattering and convenient poses. The bright young man from Arkansas didn't fail to learn the primary American lesson—the one about how the fault is never in ourselves, but always in our stars. Nor did he neglect the great good news that an American, by definition and right of birth, is always and forever innocent. Foreigners incite wars, manufacture cocaine, sponsor terrorists, and breed disease. Americans cleanse the world of its impurities. Foreigners commit crimes against humanity. Americans make well-intentioned mistakes. The fault is never one of character or motive.

What Milan Kundera identified as "the unbearable lightness of being" marked the Clinton presidency from its inception—a weightlessness associated over the last six years with the euphoric rising of the Dow Jones Industrial Average and comfortably adapted to the floating realm of images that constitutes the kingdom of celebrity. Like everything else emanating from the Clinton Administration (the futile war on drugs, the empty threatening of Saddam Hussein), the White House story of Monica Lewinsky's unrequited love presupposes a world in which words stand surrogate for deeds, where what matters is how words look and sound, not whatever it is they supposedly mean. Truth is a stage prop, like the mirrors and the palm fronds, and lying is the art of set decoration—smoothing the nouns in the briefing books, fluffing up the throw pillows and the cabinet ministers, carrying the banner of Christ or the flag of democracy into the breach of the nearest television studio.

The sequence of events that resulted in Starr's referral followed from a similarly light-minded use of words. When Paula Jones brought a frivolous lawsuit against the President of the United States, the Supreme Court unanimously concurred in the opinion that any elitist distinction between a sitting president and a Washington cabdriver was anti-democratic. Prosecutor Starr drew upon comparable lines of weightless interpretation for the money and legal authority that sustained his obsessive inspection of Clinton's soul. Summoning witnesses with the fury of a suburban Savonarola, Starr conducted a prolonged exploration in darkest Arkansas, questioning the natives about crooked bankers and painted women trailing clouds of scandal. He camped in the wilderness for four years and found not one shard of evidence with which to support his theory of graft.

The lack of proof didn't matter—not to the courts, not to the Congress or the reading public, certainly not to the news media. The humiliation of handsome Bill Clinton filled in the space previously assigned to the trial of O. J. Simpson and the death of Princess Di, and in the name of the people's right to a new headline and the next sensation, sometimes things get lost. The special prosecutor was good copy, his pinched self-righteousness opposed to stunning effect against Clinton's open-mouthed and sentimental piety. Tarantino couldn't have done it better—the moralist and the prom king, both hypocrites, both sublimely selfish, each certain of his superior virtue and one as quick as the other to exploit the instrument of Monica Lewinsky; the Old Testament against the New Testament, Texas versus Arkansas, the Big Game in the Bible Bowl.

A big story, maybe as big as the movie about the *Titanic*. So big that the Justice Department didn't have the heart to refuse

Starr the encouragement of a $40 million author's advance for rights to the hardcover and paperback editions. Nobody at the time knew what the book was about. Neither did Starr. His publishers on the House Judiciary Committee were expecting to read something about Arkansas gamblers sitting around with trailer-trash women in a spa in Hot Springs; the assignment editors at the *Wall Street Journal* and the *New York Times* hoped that at least some fragment of the Whitewater scandal, the one their papers had been promoting for the better part of four years, would, in the end, prove true.

As so often in the past, author Starr failed to deliver the manuscript specified in his contract. No gamblers; no selling of public office; no plot to murder Vincent Foster; no Colombian drug dealers or Chinese arms merchants; not even a supplementary list of Webster Hubbell's purchases from Victoria's Secret. But the special prosecutor didn't neglect his promise of a smash bestseller. Just at the moment when it looked as if he might have nothing to report, a merciful God sent him a tape recording and performed the miracle of Linda Tripp. His faithfulness rewarded, his cup overflowing with the joy of smut, Starr clapped down upon his head the helmet of remonstrance and sallied forth onto the darkling plain of the Potomac to prod his newfound band of captive witnesses (Linda and Monica and the White House secretaries) with the lance of righteousness and the sword of stern rebuke.

For the next seven months all the best people in Washington listened anxiously to the distant sound of Starr fumbling through closets, and when at last they heard the president speak, they braced themselves for the tasks of ritual purification. Fortunately

for the nation's spiritual health and safety, Washington abounds
with euphemists (journalists as well as politicians and academic
experts) as blessed as President Clinton with the talent for bleach-
ing and softening the meaning of words. Devoted to the preser-
vation of the American dream of innocence, they define the
nation's politics as a competition between different theories of
what constitutes a proper detergent, and the best of them remember always the exemplary communiqué from General William
Westmoreland, commander of American forces during the regret-
table war in Vietnam, who said of the little Vietnamese girl blaz-
ing with the light of napalm that he had been told, and so
believed, that she was burned by an hibachi stove.

Another month passed before Starr sent his report to the House
Judiciary Committee, but by late August the purifiers of the nation's conscience were already on the move, polishing the brightwork of their sanctimony, consulting with clergymen, practicing
worried frowns. Senator Joseph Lieberman (D., Conn.) appointed
himself first among the nation's laundry persons, and on September 3, six days before Starr's vans arrived on Capitol Hill, he came
timely upon the soiled character of a man whom he had known
for thirty years, informing his colleagues in the Senate that the
President's behavior had gotten out of hand, was beginning to
frighten schoolgirls and hotel maids. America owed it to the
Washington Monument—and Joe Lieberman owed it to America—to say that the President's actions were "unacceptable."

The senator spoke for nearly half an hour, appalled by the stains
on the White House towels, and he knew, both as a citizen and
a parent, that "something very sad and sordid has happened in

American life when I cannot watch the news on television with my ten-year-old daughter anymore." The thought of a little girl in Connecticut being dragged away from the sight of Peter Jennings or the killing in Albania was pretty hard to bear, just about as poignant a summing up of what had gone wrong in America as anybody had ever heard; it served as the pitch-note for the chorus of sorrowing lament that engulfed Washington as soon as Starr's report appeared on the Internet. The children, my God, what will the children think? How can we shield them from Bill's lust, Monica's cigar? The refrain echoed through the solemn chambers of the Sunday talk shows, the politicians as grave as pastors, the pastors as smooth as politicians, and nobody mentioning either the sex-education classes imposed on six year olds in public schools or the pornographic circus on cable television, available twenty-four hours a day to every second-grade student capable of pushing a button or working a touch-tone phone.

The television news programs didn't broadcast any pictures of senators scattering incense or walking around Washington with cans of room freshener, but the usual suspects rounded up for interviews delivered their sound bites in Senator Lieberman's suggested key of B flat minor—slow, nonpartisan, and unctuous—and they were careful not to say too much, not to rush to judgment, to assure the good people of America (the little girls in Iowa and Alabama as well as the ones in rural Connecticut) that as soon as all of us here in Washington had received our instructions from the opinion polls, Congress would know what to do, would move bravely and expeditiously forward into the bright, golden day of innocence regained.

*November 1998*

# *Shadowboxing*

Secrecy is as essential to Intelligence as vestments and incense
to a Mass, or darkness to a Spiritualist seance, and must
at all costs be maintained, quite irrespective of whether or not
it serves any purpose.
—Malcolm Muggeridge

N

o topic of conversation in New York these days moves more quickly to the margins of paranoia than the one about the invasions of privacy, and whether voiced by film directors at a screening in Tribeca or by bankers at dinner on Madison Avenue, the stirrings of alarm dwell on the improved means of surveillance—optic, genetic, electronic—available to the seekers-out of human weakness and moral error. The hostess describes the investigation of her first marriage by her second husband's divorce lawyers; a partner at Bear Stearns says he never carries a cell phone because of its uses as a tracking device; an apprentice celebrity mentions a rude encounter with a bald photographer. All present then proceed to further observations borrowed from their nervous reading of the news—reports of private detectives rummaging through hospital and credit-card records, references to Special Prosecutor Kenneth Starr (ominously recalled and unanimously deplored), stories about political candidates compiling "opposition research" (i.e., anthologies of campaign slander), about computer hackers breaking into the Pentagon's communications systems, corporate executives stealing data from their associates as well as from their competitors, insurance companies requiring prospective policy holders to submit samples of their DNA.

Although I never fail to sympathize with the general concern, I doubt that it's possible to engineer a happy return to a world in which secrets could be kept. I once began to count the surveillance cameras in which I make cameo appearances during the course of an ordinary day (cameras in restaurants and stores, cameras in office buildings, hotel lobbies, freight elevators, and public parks), and when by three o'clock in the afternoon I reached the number nineteen, I knew that I might as well be counting gargoyles on a medieval cathedral. Given the sophistication of the technology apt to become more sophisticated with every new generation of the microchip, the condition of privacy begins to resemble the state of Christian grace. Nobody knows for certain where, or at what moment in time, it can be said to exist.

Various government and commercial entities routinely intercept much of the daily telephone traffic traveling in and out of New York and Washington (or on any other circuit deemed worthy of notice and inspection); together with the multinational corporation in Stuttgart transferring credit to a bank in Miami, the movie star in Los Angeles relaying instructions to her dressmaker in Milan exposes nominally privileged information to peer review and public broadcast. Internet services assemble profiles of their subscribers (what they read, who they know, where they travel); satellite cameras drifting in orbit at an altitude of 1,000 miles piece together photographs of yacht basins and soccer matches, of solitary poets walking Irish roads, and of schoolchildren rolling hoops on the Ringstrasse.

How then does one learn to live in a glass house—in a world where everybody can see everybody else, if not "live and in person" at least in the pages of *People* magazine and the lighted window of *Entertainment Tonight?* I don't know of any good answer to the question, but aside from the possibilities suggested in satirical novels (among them Aldous Huxley's *Brave New World* and George Orwell's *Nineteen Eighty-Four*), I remember coming across three responses over the last twenty-odd years that I thought instructive.


First and probably foremost, the cautionary tale told by Melor Sturua, a Washington correspondent for the Soviet newspaper *Izvestia,* with whom I was briefly acquainted in the early 1980s. The Cold War was still in progress, Moscow still the seat of evil empire, and Sturua simply assumed that the KGB was keeping track of his phone calls, that secret police, were busy composing a dossier, taking clandestine photographs, adding documents to the file. If he made an important mistake, the authorities wouldn't be at a loss for a reason to send him to Siberia. In the meantime he was free to do as he pleased, and he didn't allow "the idiocy of politics" to censor his appreciation of the "superfluous luxuries" that he sometimes characterized for his readers as the proofs of "decadent capitalism." He bought his suits in London and his ties in Paris, owned a hot tub and a Chrysler convertible, delighted in supermarkets. Among the authors to whom he most often referred, he was particularly fond of quoting Talleyrand and Thomas Jefferson. Once or twice a year we met for lunch in the Madison Hotel on M Street, and Sturua took pleasure in pointing out the prominent American journalists seated in the dining room—a *New York Times* columnist, the editor of the *Washington Post,* a White House correspondent for CBS. He knew them all, not only by name but also by the sum of their indiscretions—their extramarital affairs, the sources to whom they were indebted, the confidences they had betrayed. It amused him that the American journalists didn't return the courtesy.

"Your colleagues see only celebrities," he said. "Gagarin, Brezhnev, maybe Yevtushenko."

What amused him even more was the joylessness of American tycoons, their fear of publicity and their pallid inhibitions. Here they were in the great American department store, their hands full of money and their weekends bright with toys, but they didn't know how to have a good time—plutocrats afraid of their own desires, thinking of their reputations as tablecloths on which they didn't wish to spill the soup. People in power in Russia didn't worry so much about their reputations. If they could pass the Sunday school test, they wouldn't be in power.

"Suppose a member of the Politburo gets drunk in a restaurant," Sturua once said, "so drunk that he insults a general and smashes the chandeliers. It's okay. The incident comes to the attention of the secret police, but nobody tells Ted Koppel. Same thing if the general spends a week in Yalta with four dancers from the Bolshoi. More proof of bad character, but no sheepish confession to Barbara Walters."

I said something about the oppressiveness of a regime held hostage to a system of communal blackmail. Sturua shrugged and considered the choice between the caviar and the smoked salmon.

"Like everywhere else," he said. "No society is duty-free. At the airport, yes; on earth, no."

Before Sturua returned to the Soviet Union in August of 1982, we had a last lunch together at a French restaurant on West Fifty-fifth Street, and on my way back to the office I hailed an ancient Checker cab moving cautiously south on Fifth Avenue, a tall clump of radio aerials sprouting from its roof like the antennae of an overgrown insect. The driver, heavyset and suspicious, was crowded into the front seat with enough electronic equipment to furnish a recording studio, and he didn't unlock the rear doors until he had removed his headphones and looked closely at my hands and shoes. The taxi license gave his name as Forrester, Templeton B., and before we had traveled five blocks together, he informed me that we were surrounded by enemies. New York was a dangerous city, swarming with liberals and pornographers, also with corrupt police officials, angry black people, and espionage agents headquartered at the United Nations.

Unlike Sturua, Forrester had assimilated the ethos of the Cold War, and as a defense against the spies watching his every move he sought the vast and mysterious powers of an impregnable omniscience. He wore a baseball jacket stamped with the shield of the National Rifle Association, and he had arranged his radio receivers in what I took to be some sort of military sequence. Naming each of them in turn (police, hospital, airports, outer boroughs, etc.) he brought up the volume on the different frequencies and explained what was meant by the various call signs and code numbers—". . . robbery in progress . . . four ambulances . . . fog." Two scanning devices randomly acquired nearby telephone conversations, and while we waited for the light to change at Forty-second Street, we listened to a man (older, uneasy, name unknown) arranging to meet Jessica (younger, bored, demanding "a suite, not a room") later that same afternoon at the St. Regis Hotel.

"Some days it gets real interesting," Forrester said. "Some days the fare recognizes one of the voices. Soap-opera stuff, right there in the back seat."

The soap-opera stuff nowadays appears right there on the front page of the *New York Times,* updated every three hours on the Drudge Report, and sold the next day to HBO, but I like to think of Forrester still driving his Checker cab in hostile territory (possibly on an Indian reservation or somewhere in his native Tennessee), a heroic American paranoid in the great tradition that encompasses the whispering in Richard Nixon's White House, Ronald Reagan's theory of a "Star Wars" missile defense, Oliver Stone's movies, the citizens of the Aryan Nations in Idaho, and the confidentiality agreement that Tom Cruise and Nicole Kidman require of their servants (the cook, the gardener, the secretaries) as a condition of their employment. The legal document runs to seventeen paragraphs of small print obliging the servants (on pain of swift and certain impoverishment) to keep their mouths wide shut about anything seen or heard while bringing hair dryers to the dressing tables of the entity defined as "collectively 'Cruise.' " For disclosures that appear in a newspaper or magazine, "$20 for each copy printed, with a minimum of $1,000,000 per publication"; for disclosures published in books, "$250 for each copy printed, with a minimum of $1,000,000 for publication"; for disclosures on U.S. network television, "$5,000,000 per broadcast," etc. The list proceeds through the several tiers of ancillary exhibition, including (but not limited to) video cassettes, audio records and tapes, non-network and foreign television broadcasts.

Not everyone, of course, can afford to live in the grand paranoid manner of "collectively 'Cruise,' " and although I meet a fair number of people who might wish to do so (people who refuse to own credit cards or answer any question put to them on a printed form, people who brush their teeth with bottled water, avoid the Internet, dust their windowsills for fingerprints, and test new hunting rifles by shooting at the blimps overhanging golf tournaments), few of them travel with fourteen radios. They resign themselves instead to an accommodation with what earlier centuries would have recognized as "the world at court," and for the most part they spy on themselves—careful to strike attractive poses and say nothing that might give offense. The genius of modern technology substitutes the settings of the television studio, the gossip column, and the fashion magazine for what were once the palaces at White-hall and Versailles, and in the royal apartments of celebrity, one must watch one's tongue.

The acute sense of anxiety reduces the conversation to an exchange of commonplaces both bland and small, a circumstance to which I was introduced in the early 1990s, when I conducted a television show meant to prompt lively discussion of newly published books. The show invited the author and two other guests to pursue any line of argument that came readily to mind, even to the point of strong opinion and blunt objection. The guests seldom availed themselves of the opportunity. Sometimes they made loud or churlish noises before walking onto the set, but as soon as the camera light blinked red, they spoke as calmly as funeral directors, excessively polite, as well behaved as circus dogs sitting primly erect on little wooden chairs. Similar codes of etiquette regulate most of the country's public speaking, and the general atmosphere of suffocating conformity matches the portraits of the life at court drawn by Shakespeare and Molière. The paranoia turns inward, and the courtiers who hang like acrobats from the trapeze of their connections never escape the feeling of weightlessness and dread, would-be persons of note or consequence smiling in all directions, glad to say or do whatever is required in return for a camera angle or a contribution to the alumni fund, for a page of advertising, a letter of credit, or a word of praise.

Maybe we can learn a lesson from the Russians. The recent news reports from Moscow suggest that the Soviet practice of communal blackmail has been modified to fit the new forms of free enterprise, the KGB dossiers changed into what is known as "kompromat," compromising material that everybody holds in escrow for every-body else. The Russian press makes extravagant use of the cur-rency, and every week yet another high-ranking government official fails to pass the tests of conduct and deportment—Boris Yeltsin falling down drunk on the steps of the Kremlin, Prose-cutor General Yuri Skuratov filmed in bed with two prostitutes, miscellaneous finance ministers found to have been transferring public money to their private accounts in Switzerland. But nobody goes to prison or Siberia.

If the Russians can domesticate their paranoia, conceivably we could do the same. Remove the Christmas wrappings of Puritan inhibition and Victorian restraint, and the invasions of privacy might reveal the American spirit of adventure that so many of our social critics have given up for lost—actors recounting scenes of barbarian depravity, politicians speaking golden truths, corpora-tion presidents carrying sword canes and pillaging Caribbean sugar islands. No longer pressed to invent their material, the au-thors of celebrity profiles might discover stories worth the telling. The tabloids would never lack for genuinely sensational headlines, and as a society we might crawl out from under the blanket of warm and welcome lies.

The hypothesis succeeds in theory but probably not in fact. As both Tocqueville and Sturua noticed on their tours of the United States, the Americans don't have much of a talent for living large and dramatic lives, a timid people disinclined to exercise their well-advertised freedoms of speech, too many of them too afraid of not being asked to dance. Open the national vault of sexual and financial secrets, and most of them would prove worthless and dull, as harmless as the Wizard of Oz, embarrassingly empty of the power to sell papers, inspire awe, attract photographers, instill fear. Which is possibly why we prefer the fanciful conspiracy theory to the plain and disappointingly unblemished fact. Our beloved paranoia protects us from the awful news that we might not be as interesting as we like to think.

*September 1999*

# Compass Bearings

To the child, the savage and the Wall Street operator everything
seems possible, hence their credulity.
                    —ERIC HOFFER

*E*ver since the Enron Corporation disappeared early last
winter in a cloud of shredded paper, the promoters of the
faith in fairy gold have been staging a diligent search for
the fabulous instrument known to President George W. Bush and
the editors of the *Wall Street Journal* as America's lost "ethical
compass." Although nobody could say for certain what the thing
looks like, or whether it was first seen aboard the U.S.S. *Constitution* in the spring of 1812 or somewhere on the field at Gettysburg in the summer of 1863, everybody knew that it was very
precious and very old, that it points corrupt accountants in the
direction of the nearest church, leads irresponsible corporate executives away from the temptation of low-cost stock options,
guides the United States Air Force to noncivilian targets in Central Asia.

The first search parties that set forth in late January were small

and not yet desperate (a few senior money managers concerned
about the sluggish performance of the equity markets, three or
four elderly economists consulting maps and the notebooks of
John Maynard Keynes); by the last week in July the Dow Jones
industrial average was down 2,300 points, and what had begun
as a tentative exploration had become a massive Easter egg hunt
joined by several thousand volunteers—politicians armed with
subpoenas, lawyers bearing lanterns, eminent historians quoting
the aphorisms of Ronald Reagan, a rabble of television cameramen
and FBI agents struggling with dogs. The gathering of so large a
host spoke to the increasingly forlorn hope of finding the financial
equivalent of true north, also to the even more pressing need to
preserve the belief that God wants every good American to become
as rich as Bill and Melinda Gates. The Enron bankruptcy had been
followed by the demolition of Arthur Andersen and the wreck of
Global Crossing, and for the next six months every day's dawn
brought word of something else gone rotten in one or another of
the country's corporate boardrooms, the loss of shareholder assets
indicating levels of fraud, stupidity, and greed all too easily mea-
sured by a desolate set of numbers:

| Company | Percentage Change in Share Price Since 1/14/00 |
| --- | --- |
| Global Crossing | −99.9 |
| WorldCom | −99.8 |
| Enron | −99.8 |
| Adelphia | −99.8 |
| MicroStrategy | −99.1 |

| Lucent Technologies | −99.4 |
| KMart | −91 |
| Qwest Communications | −88.4 |
| AOL Time Warner | −81.5 |
| Xerox | −67.5 |
| Halliburton | −56.5 |
| Tyco International | −55.2 |
| ImClone Systems | −52.3 |

The numbers supplied the bleak outline of the story; the tabloid press filled out the narrative with lurid anecdote—swinish executives paying themselves salaries of $150 million a year as a reward for destroying the business and watering the company stock; Merrill Lynch fined $100 million for milking its customers with self-serving lies; crooked auditors setting up dummy corporations as hollow as Hollywood movie sets; countless employees discarded as carelessly as gum wrappers, robbed of their savings and their pensions; the Xerox Corporation padding its revenues by the comfortable margin of $2 billion, countless investors shorn like sheep or peeled like grapes.

Sure that the missing compass was there somewhere, carelessly misplaced by a clerk in Alan Greenspan's office or temporarily on loan from the Library of Congress, the search parties in the months of April and May chased down leads in cyberspace, convened

congressional investigative committees, sent scouts to make dis-
creet inquiries of the offshore tax havens in Bermuda and the
Cayman Islands. More than once they came upon what they proclaimed to be the threshold of discovery; they lowered floodlights,
called in the ambulances, hugged one another with shouts and
tears of joy. Their despair was awful to behold when, on opening
the bank vault or turning over the rock, out crawled a grinning
Martha Stewart or a wet-nosed L. Dennis Kozlowski with a golf
ball in his mouth.

No more than a year had passed since the nation's business
leaders had been seen as godlike figures descending from corporate
helicopters as if from Mt. Olympus, but the long season of heavy
rain in Wall Street had changed a good many princes back into
frogs. The editors at *Fortune* and *Business Week* preferred the term
"bad apples" (a few of which must be expected to fall from even
the healthiest of trees); if a collapsed stock price couldn't be at-
tributed to thievery or fraud, the magazines depicted the chief
executive officer as a well-meaning but bewildered fool, helpless
in the hands of charlatans (invariably younger men, arrogant and
cruel) who mystified the old gent with charts he didn't know how
to read and Russian girls whose language he didn't understand.
The sudden turning of once gilt-edged names to mud (among
them Kenneth Lay, A. Alfred Taubman, and Gary Winnick) followed from the recognition that folly is easier to excuse than crime
and supported the theory developed nearly fifty years ago by the
economist John Kenneth Galbraith to account for the stock market crash of 1929. Bubbles float and bubbles burst, said Galbraith,
and in both good times and bad American corporations hold "an

inventory of undiscovered embezzlement . . . it should perhaps be called the bezzle." When money is plentiful and cheap, the Bezzle grows; when "money is watched with a narrow, suspicious eye," commercial morality improves, and "the Bezzle shrinks." The *Wall Street Journal* endorsed the explanation; so did the Business Roundtable, the banking committees of Congress, and every retail broker licensed to sell raffle tickets on the New York Stock Exchange. Why yes, of course, the Bezzle—the Bezzle, a few bad apples, and every now and then an imbecile in the chairman's office practicing his putting stroke; join these unfortunate circumstances with the occasional run of plain bad luck, and we have the answer, all too human and perfectly understandable, for the otherwise inexplicable loss of moral direction.

Which is where the quest for the fabled compass might have been abandoned had it not been for the simple error in arithmetic reported on June 25 by the management of WorldCom, Inc. The company accountants somehow had confused earnings with operating expenses, with the result that its balance sheets over the last two years attested to the presence of nonexistent revenues in the amount of $3.8 billion. The chief executive officer didn't fail to issue the customary expression of complete surprise, but the stock price reacted poorly (off 200 points in the next twenty-four hours), and the childish simplicity of the scam (no mail drop in Switzerland, no complex maze of fictional transaction; not even a holiday distribution of bribes to government officials in Washington or Jackson, Mississippi) compounded the injury of a crime with the rudeness of an insult. Learned doctors of capitalist philosophy discerned symptoms of popular mistrust possibly dangerous not only to the body but also to the spirit of the national economy; they warned of "a deadly threat to public confidence" and observed that "it was not enough to trust to the innate honesty of the brokerage community." Senators both Republican and Democratic rushed to the microphones on Capitol Hill to insist that "people go to jail." Paul Volcker, former chairman of the Federal Reserve, appeared on C-SPAN's *Washington Journal* and ABC's *Nightline* to say that the country's economic engine needs clean filters; Paul O'Neill, the secretary of the treasury, advocated the public hanging of criminal chief financial officers "from the very highest branches"; Henry A. McKinnell, vice-chairman of the Business Roundtable, cautioned against the making of foolish generalizations on the evidence of "eight or ten companies who allegedly behaved in ways that are incomprehensible . . . and deserve what they're getting." The dean of a business school in Maryland informed the cameras from PBS that his students would be taking field trips to nearby prisons, there to hear the confessions of businessmen doing time on various counts of racketeering—to hear their confessions, learn from their mistakes, take heart from their acts of penance and contrition.

The fanfare of indignant outrage and the chorus of bland reassurance served as overture to President Bush's coming to the wicked city of New York on July 9 to make the crooked straight and the rough places plain. Before a crowd of wealthy pharisees assembled in the ballroom of the Regent Wall Street Hotel, the President dressed up his remarks in the language of a sermon and placed a wreath of platitudes at the golden feet of Mammon. "The business pages of American newspapers should not read like a scandal sheet," he said; the time had come to "usher in a new era of integrity in corporate America," to "end the days of cooking the books, shading the truth," to know and remember that "there is no capitalism without conscience; there is no wealth without character."

The President's tone was unctuous and firm, his manner similar to that of a television evangelist recalling the faithful to the paths of righteousness. Together with threats of punishment ("the full weight of the law" deployed to "expose and root out corruption," longer jail sentences for wayward executives, the Securities and Exchange Commission to be equipped with a strike force comparable to a police department SWAT team, etc.) he distributed uplifting thoughts and earnest exhortations:

Corporate America must learn to distinguish between "ambition and destructive greed," to inspire trust and promote transparency, to show God and Paul Volcker that markets "can be both dynamic and honest."

"Our schools of business must be principled teachers of right and wrong and not surrender to moral confusion and relativism."

Good corporate citizens must "set a moral tone by showing their disapproval" of bad corporate citizens.

Careful not to mention any names, either of individuals or corporations, the President spoke for nearly half an hour, and for the first twenty minutes it was possible to think that he was addressing his remarks to the Liberty Bell or to the Washington Monument, the words meant to be appreciated as ceremonial salutes fired from a battery of Civil War cannons. They drifted across the podium like puffs of smoke, and to try to invest them with meaning was to be asked to believe that Mr. Bush knows nothing about the history of the United States, the temperament of the American people, the workings of capitalism, or the sources of his own fortune. How else does the federal government compose its budget if not by "cooking the books"; by what means other than "shading the truth" does anybody sell a car, a parcel of real estate, or a politician? Begin the story of America's triumphs with Thomas Jefferson's dictum that "money, not morality, is the principle of commercial nations" and where in the record of the last 200 years do we find much evidence to refute the proposition? In the gallery of national heroes who stands higher in the hearts and minds of their countrymen than the grand predators descending in the long line of criminal succession from the earliest fur traders selling liquor to the Indians, to the land speculators moving west in the 1840s with the hope that they could "get in, get rich, and get out," to the late-nineteenth-century Wall Street financiers (among them John D. Rockefeller, Cornelius Vanderbilt, and J. P. Morgan) of whom it was said, usually with envy and admiration, "When they speak they lie, and when they are silent, they are stealing?" How else did Mr. Bush acquire both a baseball team and the office of the presidency if not as gifts from self-interested corporate executives unable to detect a significant difference between "ambition and destructive greed"? If not with the promise of "something for nothing," who would know how to monetize the great truth that every true American is entitled to everything he or she can get away with?

What was impressive about the President's speech was the way in which he managed to sustain the tone of disappointment and surprise ("We've learned of some business leaders obstructing justice . . . problems long in the making and now coming to light. . . . We've learned of CEOs earning tens of millions of dollars in bonuses just before their companies go bankrupt. Before he reached his peroration I understood that he had adopted the familiar persona of the idiot CEO—the President of the United States revealed as just another good-natured, holy fool, a block of polished wood at the head of the boardroom table, helpless in the hands of charlatans (irresponsible and un-American) who mystified the SEC with numbers that not even Vice President Dick Cheney could understand.

The line of argument didn't inspire confidence among the bond brokers in the ballroom, but neither did it evoke laughter, and it was not without its uses or its merits. Who else but such a president, as guileless as the unicorn and as innocent as Forrest Gump, could have retrieved the fabled ethical compass from the swamps of moral confusion and the wilderness of debt? And where, pray tell, did he stumble upon the precious object for which so many others had searched so long in vain? Why, nowhere else but in the breasts of "the leaders in this room." It had been there all along, hidden in their compensation packages, and if only they would take the trouble to read the small print, they would know that the nation respects them not for their wealth but for their integrity, and that they had it in their power "to restore the people's trust in American business."

Wonderful and important news, of course, but the stock market was slow to grasp its significance, and it arrived too late to rescue the mathematicians at WorldCom from the pit of relativism. The Dow Jones industrial average dropped another 1,500 points during the ten trading days subsequent to the President's speech, and on July 21 WorldCom declared a $107 billion bankruptcy, the largest number ever posted on the leader board of American entrepreneurship. Fortunately for the health of the republic, the responsible corporate executives who heard the speech recognized the long-term benefits certain to accrue from the safe return of the virtuous compass. Larry Johnston, chief executive officer of a supermarket chain in Idaho, spoke for the grateful majority of his peers when he told the *New York Times* that Mr. Bush "hit the nail on the head. . . . He stood up as CEO of this country and said the whole issue of integrity needs to be higher on the scale of awareness." Equally relieved to know that what was lost had now been found, the editors of the *Wall Street Journal* were quick to point out that American businessmen, having regained the instrument of moral navigation, once again were capable of regulating themselves, without the interference of Washington politicians determined to sap the energy of the free-enterprise system by writing ignorant and restrictive laws. But in all the happy throng rejoicing in the President's discovery, the happiest of all were the generals at the Pentagon planning the invasion of Iraq. It's no good going to war without an ethical compass. The Navy shells the wrong beaches, the Army doesn't know which Arabs to shoot, the Air Force bombs targets cluttered with the low-yield nuisance of civilians.

*September 2002*

# When in Rome

The road of excess leads to the palace of wisdom.
—WILLIAM BLAKE

During the months prior to last November's congressional elections the apostles of American empire tended to confine their enthusiasms to foreign-policy journals funded by the reactionary heirs to handsome beer or real-estate fortunes. It wasn't that the voices in the prophetic wilderness doubted the truth of their revelation. Only a blind Arab could fail to notice the weight of the country's military power or the scale of its economy, but the blunt statement of imperialist purpose risked the raising of alarm among voters still attached to their belief in such a thing as a democratic republic. Although both harmless and naive, the belief retained a sentimental value within the history departments of obscure New England universities, and why bother to disturb people content with their keepsake memories of Thomas Jefferson and the comforts of their colonial pewter?

The election results opened the envelopes of candor. The Republican Party added the capture of the Congress to its possession of the White House and the Supreme Court, thus shifting the de facto imbalance of power further to the evangelical right; soon afterward the United Nations resolved to disarm Saddam Hussein on terms encompassing the submission of the Security Council to the will of the United States. Even the blind Arabs could read the handwriting on the palace wall, and the prophets of the Pax Americana issued forth into the light of the received wisdom. By the time the balloons were in the streets for the Macy's Thanksgiving Day Parade, they were giving interviews to *Time* magazine, touring the television talk-show circuit with their collection of analogies between the glory of the Bush Administration and the grandeur that was Rome. The good news was not slow in coming to the conference rooms in Washington and the dinner tables of New York. State Department functionaries studying trays of smoked salmon spoke of sending the 82nd Airborne Division to punish insolent barbarians not only in the deserts of Mesopotamia but also in the forests of Illyricum and the mountains of Cyrene; patrician lawyers gazing from high windows into the darkness of Central Park mentioned the imminent passage of new federal regulations (apropos the penal system and the tax code) intended to impose on America's plebeian rabble a long-overdue regime change equivalent to the military occupation of Iraq; trend-setting publishers in Greenwich Village, alert to a revived interest in the Emperor Caesar Augustus, commissioned new biographies amplifying Edward Gibbon's compliment to "the sublime perfections of an Eternal Parent and an Omnipotent Monarch."

Like everybody else with any sense, and never having been one

to question the splendor of the Fifth Fleet or to resist the deifi-
cation of Ronald Reagan and Bill Gates, I was glad to see so many
people awakened to the prospect of a noble destiny. Even so, and
without meaning to revise (much less disparage or contradict) anybody's hope of an empire worthy of a word from Tacitus, I cannot
help but think that we have yet to reach the zenith of our tri-
umph. I don't quarrel with the fact that the country has made
steady and impressive progress toward the valor of the Caesars and
the piety of the Antonines, but I worry that we might be a trifle
early with the distribution of the laurel leaves and the hymn to
Capitoline Jupiter. We have done much; we can do more. We
understand the technology; we have yet to acquire the proper aesthetic and the preferred habit of mind. Fortunately we are Americans, an inventive and self-improving people, and I know that I
can count on the wise and careful reader not to mistake a few
helpful suggestions for niggling complaints or unproductive criticism.

## CLASS DISTINCTIONS

Certainly we have made a good beginning, and I don't think
it too presumptuous to say that no other nation in the history of
the world has engineered so massive a transfer of wealth with so
little bloodshed in so short a space of time. It's only been twenty
years since Ronald Reagan first came to the White House with
the promise of a bright new morning in America, and except for
a few discredited columnists in the ruins of the leftist press, I
know of nobody who can quibble with what has been accomplished—80 percent of the nation's property now securely in the

hands of 10 percent of the population, our 13,000 richest families possessed of a net worth equivalent to the assets owned by the country's 20 million poorest families, our ten most highly paid CEOs earning an average of $154 million a year as opposed to the mere pittance of $3.5 million in 1981.

The numbers speak to the presence of what the old Romans would have recognized as an equestrian class composed of individuals sanctified with a capital worth of 400,000 sesterces and thus entitled to the privileges of social distinction, political office, and military rank. Accustomed to the standard shows of deference that every decent society awards to the human forms of money (togas made of silk instead of wool, fawning barbers, rooms furnished with sandalwood and fretted ivory), even the most ignoble of the Romans didn't rest content with the meager arts of acquisition. They enjoyed the taste and sight of blood. More theatrical in character than our own corporate optimates, not as anxious as our Hollywood celebrities about the keeping up of bourgeois appearances, they found time in their busy schedules to poison their husbands, banish their wives, torture their slaves. When compelled to display the ornaments of their vanity they didn't sponsor golf tournaments or buy another beachfront house in Florida; they drank wine distilled from pearls, dined on peacocks and flamingos, presented matchless gifts (1,000 captive Gauls, 4,000 singing Christians, 2,000 troubled Jews) to the animals in the Colosseum.

## COMMERCE

Devoted to the theory of free markets but contemptuous of clerks and bored by the dreary shuffling of numbers, the ancient

Romans derived their wealth from the honest labor of the imperial legions. Straightforward conquest, summary execution, remorseless plunder.

The recent reports from our own financial frontiers indicate a profound appreciation of the classical style, and because our business community seems well on its way to establishing a criminal elite, I hesitate to suggest further refinements when so many capable and intelligent people obviously have been devoting so much of their valuable time and effort to the project. The available evidence seeping into the newspapers over the last twelve months describes a full range of home-delivered fraud—reliable flows of false information (from senior management to the audit committee, from the audit committee to senior management), bogus stock trades, counterfeit balance sheets, off-shore tax shelters, insider trading, systematic theft, generous distributions of interest-free loans and golf-club memberships to favored friends and sycophants; I think we can rely on the assumption that our most innovative and forward-thinking corporations know how to rob an investor, cheat a stockholder, corrupt an orphan. But so did a good many of the merchants known to Alexander Hamilton, as well as most of the speculators synonymous with our happy remembrance of both "The Roaring Twenties" and "The Gilded Age." In other words, and once again without wishing to withhold credit where credit is due, we still stand on the threshold of renown. Our success in the drug and weapons trades has taught us to devalue the commodity of human life; the placing of our health-care services at the disposal of insurance companies has improved our understanding of the profits to be realized from the happy marriage

of mortal suffering with immortal avarice. Great strides, magnificent achievements, but well within the tradition of our own commercial history. Not yet the grandeur that was Rome.

Which probably is why I read with heavy heart the newspaper
stories about Jack Welch, the former chairman of General Electric,
spending $13,000 a month for French wine, flowers, and new
shoes, or Tyco's L. Dennis Kozlowski assigning to his conglom-
erate the cost of a $15,000 umbrella stand, or Winona Ryder
stealing a $2,000 dress from a store in Beverly Hills. The sums
are paltry, the crimes empty of romance. When the newspapers
make a show of moral outrage about Lizzie Grubman dispersing
a crowd of vulgar commoners with the assistance of her SUV (killing nobody, merely showing off the beauty of her designer jeans),
I think of the Emperor Nero, also costumed in a workman's rags,
making his mischievous evening rounds of the Roman taverns,
sometimes surprising the company by stabbing to death one or
two of the patrons seated incautiously near the door. The emperor
also liked to loot the shops below the Palatine and Aventine hills.
Bringing the stolen goods back to the palace, he sold them at
auction to those of his courtiers carelessly in attendance on his
triumphant return, bidding up to 100,000 sesterces the price of
a thimble or a comb; to the buyers forced into instant penury,
Nero sometimes offered what his uncle Caligula considered an
amusing but prudent choice—the debt excused and half of the
courtier's estate allowed to pass unmolested to his children on
condition that he promptly commit suicide. The other half of the
estate the emperor reserved to his own use. Always short of money
and not inclined to give fund-raising speeches, he adopted the

practice of whimsical confiscation, seizing the property of wealthy citizens in whom he discovered a flaw of character, an irritating mannerism, or an unwillingness to listen to him play the flute. To newly appointed magistrates charged with the cultivation of the imperial revenue, Nero condescended to offer only one sentence of advice, "You and I must see that nobody is left with anything." The Enron Corporation applied the same principle to its employees, its stockholders, and its pensioners, but the interoffice email announcing bankruptcy or dismissal lacked Nero's gift for phrase.

## DISSENT

As compared to the Romans during the reigns of both the Julian and the Flavian emperors, I'm afraid that we still have much to learn about the regulation of seditious speech. Not that we haven't identified the impediment to the tranquillity of government and to the repose of a virtuous people "well supplied with luxuries and accustomed to defeat." Vigilant librarians everywhere in the country refuse to disseminate the works of Mark Twain; the doctrines of political correctness defend the pages of our better newspapers against the advance of incendiary adjectives and rebellious nouns; the Justice Department's supervision of our mail and telephone communications insures a decent respect, if not for the opinion of mankind, at least for the opinion of Attorney General John Ashcroft.

All well and good and pointed in the right direction, but still by way of preamble to what remains to be achieved. So careful were the voices in the presence of an emperor that most of what

·

was said aspired to the silence signifying awe. Suetonius mentions an historian who characterized Caesar's assassins, Brutus and Cassius, as "the last of the Romans." The historian was executed without delay, his books destroyed, his body flung into the Tiber. Competitions in Latin prose held in the amphitheater at Lyons required the losing contestants to erase their writing with their tongues; authors too slow to make the correction were decapitated and flung into the Rhone.

If our own responsible authorities haven't yet acquired the knack of flinging rude journalists into the Hudson or the Potomac, at least we can take heart from the servility of the Washington correspondents who submit their questions as if on tufted pillows as well as from the routine courtesy extended to celebrities in all ranks (actresses, baseball players, CEOs) wishing to decide which of their photographs should appear on the cover of a news or fashion magazine. Another few years and we can expect our boldface names to exhibit the refinement of Caligula. The emperor worried about his overly active growth of body hair. If in his presence a courtier made the mistake of letting slip the word "goat"—no matter what the context, reference, or declension—that courtier didn't live long enough to reconsider the remark.

LICENTIOUSNESS

With regard to every other manifestation of an imperial sensibility—selfishness, pride, greed, cruelty, gluttony, and sloth—we've shown ourselves blessed, or proved ourselves equipped, with the right stuff. If we haven't fully exploited all the opportunities open to a self-confident ruling class, at least we've seen the omens and know them to be favorable.

But toward the lewd and perfumed heights of Roman orgy our progress has been hesitant and slow. Although the tabloid press brings news of scandalous Hollywood divorce, and the pornographic-film industry supplies the nation's hotel rooms with previews of the Muslim paradise, we seem to be losing ground, becoming as prudish as the Chatti or the Parthians. From the playgrounds of scented indolence on Capitol Hill and Manhattan's Upper East Side we hear nothing except occasional reports of small-time lust as ineffectual as Jack Welch's pursuit of eternal adolescence or as clumsy as President Clinton's embrace of Monica Lewinsky's blue dress.

Again I don't wish to be critical, but if we seriously aspire to the ancient Roman style, our public schools might want to consider replacing the auditorium portraits of Abraham Lincoln with those of Caligula (who seduced his sisters in the presence of his wife), of Messalina (an empress endowed with so ravenous a sexual appetite that she was capable of welcoming in a single night every member of the Praetorian Guard), of Nero, an emperor for all occasions who never fails to provide the moral of an uplifting tale. Whenever he floated on his barge across the bay at Baiae, or down the Tiber from Rome to Ostia, he found the shoreline brightened with rows of temporary brothels in which noble ladies (wives of senators, jeweled courtesans, occasionally his mother) applauded the music of his voice and solicited the favor of his person.

*       *       *

I know that we still harbor skeptics in our midst, people who say that we'll never make the grade, that no matter how many barbarians we slaughter in Iraq, or how many of our citizens we reduce to a complacent mob, we'll never live to see Nero's hospitality tents among the cherry trees beside the blue Potomac. I've heard their arguments and listened to their disappointments—too many of the nation's black people not yet in prison or the army, the oil fields of Central Asia still in the hands of barbarous tribes, the Supreme Court not yet staffed with temple priests, and our president still forced to endure the indignity of election—but I think they speak too soon. They remind me of sullen liberals unwilling to acknowledge the greatness of the American spirit or the wonders of American industry and enterprise. Give us a little time, possibly the guidance of experts assembled by the Kennedy School of Government, and who knows what we might not yet accomplish? In the forecourt of his palace Nero placed an immense statue of himself, 120 feet high, all of it in bronze. Surely we can do better—an immense statue in the open space at Ground Zero, 220 feet high, all of it in gold, dedicated to whichever corporate sponsor or hero of the gossip columns bids the winning price.

*January 2003*

# Curtain Calls

Prepare the couch; call for wine; crown thyself with roses;
perfume thyself; the god bids thee remember death.
—MARTIAL

*B*y noon on Sunday, July 18, four days before the burial at sea, the death and transfiguration of John F. Kennedy Jr. was already old news. The story line hadn't changed since early Saturday morning (the plane missing, the Coast Guard looking for it, the passengers presumed lost), but the television coverage had been virtually continuous for twenty-eight hours on all three networks and all five news channels, and the program directors had exhausted their stocks of tragic sentiment and pious film montage. No angle had been ignored, no cliché left unexamined or unexpressed, nobody who hadn't said goodbye to America's Prince. Aviation experts had been consulted, Barbara Walters had rummaged through the closet of the Kennedy family's sexual confusion, and Dan Rather had wiped away his tears; gossip columnists had placed wreaths of brave remembrance on the altar of departed glory; historians had recalled the kingdom that once was Camelot.

Everything had been done that could be done, but the plane was still missing, and the anchorpersons didn't know what else to say. The time had come to talk of other things, preferably one's self, and for the next four days, while the flags were being lowered to half-staff at Hyannis Port and the teddy bears propped up on the sidewalk in Tribeca, the conversation turned to the happier memories of those still present—old college acquaintances, once-upon-a-time kayaking companions, doe-eyed journalists—who had known John Kennedy (or if not John Kennedy, then his sister or his dog) in the dear old days when everybody was young and beautiful and pleased to be counted among the friends and guests, the very important friends and guests, on the sailboat or the lawn.

The self-promotions carried forward into print. Introducing Monday's commemorative issue of *Time* magazine, the managing editor, Walter Isaacson, remembered having had lunch with Kennedy at "a tiny Thai restaurant" in Manhattan, just the two of them, talking about fame and destiny. Elsewhere in the magazine Lance Morrow mentioned an intimate dinner at which Kennedy had discussed Egypt and *The English Patient*; Roger Rosenblatt met Kennedy once at Hickory Hill, a family stronghold in Virginia, where he learned, firsthand among the footballs and the celery rémoulade, that "when a Kennedy smiles, the world smiles back, whether it wants to or not"; Peggy Noonan saw Kennedy the day before he disappeared, thinking to herself, "What a star, a natural star . . . King Arthur's son." Similarly fond recollections appeared in every magazine that could reach the newsstand with a special edition, the eulogists quoting Sophocles and John Milton, reminded not only of King Arthur's son but also of Telemachus, Adonis, and Agamemnon, not forgetting to count themselves among the happy few on whom Kennedy once had cast the blessing of his countenance.

The complaints began to be heard on Wednesday, and at first I was surprised both by their tone and by their broad distribution among people of different ages, temperaments, and political beliefs. The news media were still doing their usual swell job of marketing dead celebrity as live product (the plane found in 116 feet of water, the pilot's competence called into question, more grief-stricken relatives), and yet here were people who already had seen enough—literary academics scornful of the futile search for Shakespearean significance, high-minded journalists who begrudged the attention being given to the story, the coverage deemed overwrought, excessive, almost vulgar. What was surprising was the note of resentment in their voices, but it wasn't until Friday, the day of the memorial service in New York City, that I understood the nature of the general objection. I happened to be having lunch with the manager of a Wall Street hedge fund, a man of no small ego, dressed by Rolex and Ermenegildo Zegna and accustomed to betting $20 million on the movement of the Korean won. He put the matter as plainly as it could be put.

"What is this American royalty crap?" he said. "And who are the Kennedys that they deserve so goddamn much attention?"

The note of envy in his voice was as unmistakable as it had

been in the voices of the self-regarding journalists, but he owned houses in California and Hawaii (a man worth $100 million after all, a friend of Arnold Schwarzenegger's), and so he didn't bang his spoon on the table, didn't cry out in the wilderness of indifferent Mexican waiters, "Yes, but what about me?"

An admirable show of restraint, I thought, worthy of an ancient Roman. With some difficulty we managed to change the subject, but I knew that he wasn't having an easy time of it—on the television screen behind the bar women with flowers in their hands were praying on the beach at Martha's Vineyard—and so while we spoke of Tiger Woods and Alan Greenspan, I wondered how it might be possible to appease his vanity. Why should he settle for an obituary when he so obviously deserved a headline? No reason. No reason at all. The news media define death as a competitive consumer good, and why shouldn't an enterprising undertaker do the same? Make death as glamorous a product as haute couture or the Academy Awards, and who knows what fortunes might be gained, what benefits bestowed on a grateful populace that reveres the transformation of flesh into property as sublime apotheosis—ballplayer into T-shirt, actress into perfume, parent into trust fund?

Maybe the country lacks an adequate supply of sacrificial kings, but it makes good the shortage with a surfeit of celebrities and a glut of billionaires. Wonderfully expensive people, eager to see their names in light, each and every one of them a match for any Kennedy. And why should they die obscure deaths in cold and anonymous hospital rooms, as if they were mere nobodies? Surely they would welcome an exit strategy both dignified and entertaining, a last hurrah agreeable to the primetime audience and flattering to the sense of self?

Name the company "Curtain Calls" or "Apotheosis, Ltd.," and the catalogue, as tastefully printed as the ones issued by Saks Fifth Avenue or the Norwegian Cruise Line, might list the available deaths under the headings "Historical," "Literary," "Cinematic," each of them accompanied by a glamorous illustration and a half-page of cheerful and reassuring prose:

---

### THE SOCRATES

*"A quiet leave-taking for serene and philosophical individuals no longer deceived by the vanity of human wishes. Convenient to both indoor and outdoor settings."*

### THE MARIE ANTOINETTE

*"A famously dramatic exit, recommended to the flamboyant and extroverted personality who delights in astonishing her friends and loved ones."*

### THE ALEXANDER HAMILTON

*"The civic-minded gentleman will find at least one of his acquaintances glad to lend a hand as surrogate for Aaron Burr."*

### THE TITANIC

*"A romantic aloha, offered only once a year, in early April, for large groups of trusted friends who share an appreciation for Old World luxury and a love of the sea."*

---

Although most patrons probably would choose to associate themselves with royalty ("The Anne Boleyn," "The Princess Di"), a number of other historical stagings might prove popular ("The Joan of Arc," "The Abraham Lincoln," "The Nelson Rockefeller"); so also, among the fictional possibilities, "The Anna Karenina," "The Ahab," "The Little Nell," "The Jay Gatsby," "The Sonny Corleone."

All superb selections, of course, made to order and designed to satisfy the most discriminating taste. "The Ahab" surely would attract a following among serious environmentalists, "The Julius Caesar" among literary intellectuals with a refined sense of irony. White sperm whales might not be easy to come by, especially during the summer months off the New England coast, but in no season would it be difficult to recruit eight or nine novelists willing to stab to death, at a moment's notice and free of charge, another writer of their own age whose book remained on the *New York Times* bestseller list for longer than two weeks.

The announcement of the company's initial stock offering almost certainly would raise moral as well as legal questions, and would-be investors could expect a period of preliminary quibbling in the churches and the courts, also indignant speeches in Congress and forceful protests from the American Medical Association. Fortunately for all concerned, the news and entertainment media establish the order of the nation's priorities, and eventually their interest would prevail. Television knows no higher form of dramatic art than death as live broadcast, and the industry apologists can be relied upon to make the inspirational arguments—the

American people ennobled by frequent proofs of courage, relieved not only of boredom but also of their hypochondria and chronic fear of extinction, their knowledge of history and literature improved by regular exposure to some of the greatest human stories ever told.

The production contract for a "Glorious Goodbye" undoubtedly would run to many pages of small print, guaranteeing various intensities of media coverage, distinguishing between different classes of service, specifying the various arrangements for supporting cast, for the refreshments and the souvenirs. "The Marie Antoinette," for instance, could be performed in Yankee Stadium in the presence of a jeering mob, or modestly at home in Southampton in front of a few invited guests; if at Southampton, some sort of permit presumably would be required from the town council; if at the stadium, some sort of agreement with George Steinbrenner about the rights to the billboard advertising on the guillotine. The disposition of the subsidiary rights would need to account not only for film and music video but also for the market in instant relics—fragments of the car wreck, wisps of blood-stained lace, the fatal cup.

Anticipating points certain to be raised by the lawyers or the publicity people, I made a list of amenities likely to be offered at additional cost:

---

### PAPARAZZI
*On foot: $6,000 (for a party of twelve)*
*On motorcycles: $12,000*

NAVAL VESSELS
*Admiral's launch: $50,000*
*(by the day)*
*Destroyer: $200,000 (by the hour)*

CATCH IN THE THROAT
*By Barbara Walters: $100,000*
*(for a suite of four)*

GRIEF-STRICKEN COUSINS
*$50 (the pair)*

MILITARY COSTUMES
*Roman: $100 (various colors)*
*Napoleonic: $500 (mostly hats)*
*Nazi German: $25,000*
*(Waffen SS)*

RENDING OF GARMENTS
*By the editors of* Time *magazine:*
*$300 (by the yard)*

METAPHORS
*By the editors of* Time *magazine:*
*$300 (by the adjective)*

SONG

*By Franz Schubert: $3,000*
*By Elton John: $300,000*

TEARS

*By Dan Rather: $5,000 (per tear)*

Large-scale productions requiring the supplementary deaths of other people ("The Romeo and Juliet," "The George A. Custer") would present legal questions for which the Supreme Court might be slow to establish clear precedents, but most of the obstacles probably could be overcome by generous distributions of cash. Custer made his last stand at the Little Big Horn with a troop of 250 cavalrymen, in the Big Sky country of Montana now fashionable among our own latter-day heroes of the western plains, among them Ted Turner, Charles Schwab, and Ralph Lauren. Should any one of those gentlemen choose to depart under the flags of freedom, I'm sure that he wouldn't begrudge generous considerations to the heirs of the doomed volunteers. Assume that most of the men in the ranks would be illegal immigrants, convicts serving life sentences, or welfare recipients burdened with incurable disease, and it could be argued that their loss was the country's gain. The National Park Service shouldn't have much trouble rounding up an impressive number of interested Native Americans; the afternoon's excitement would draw a paying crowd at least as large as the ones attending major golf tournaments; the network lucky enough to acquire the broadcast rights could sell the commercial segments to Chevrolet trucks and the National Rifle Association; the gift shop could look forward to a brisk demand for empty shell casings and broken arrows.

Smaller and more exclusive entertainments might serve as fund-raising events in the manner of museum or theater benefits. The patron donates his or her death to a blameless cause, everybody enjoys a convivial evening at the Waldorf-Astoria or the New York Public Library, somebody suitably important offers a memorable toast (prices available on request), the patron slits his or her wrist at the head table, calmly bleeding to death in a golden bowl (courtesy of Cartier or Harry Winston), while the company grieves and Pavarotti sings. The more costly the substance consumed, the larger the contribution to charity, the bolder the headlines, the more beautiful the mystery of transcendence.

Once deemed socially de rigueur, the farewell banquets should encourage heroic feats of conspicuous consumption on the part of philanthropists (statesmen and movie stars as well as the merely rich) wishing to make a last favorable impression on Liz Smith and their fellow Americans. Who could display the best linen, provide the finest Damascus steel, shed the most blood? Who could afford "The Pearl Harbor," or was daring enough to make the fashion statement implicit in "The Jesus of Nazareth"?

A marvelous attitude, of course, consistent with the healthy spirit of competitive enterprise that makes the country great, but possibly conducive to frantic scenes—the one in which the woman who has planned for "The Anna Karenina" discovers that Mrs. Astor has selected "The Catherine the Great," or the awful moment in which Donald Trump's accountant tells him that he can afford "The Jack Ruby" or "The Lee Harvey Oswald" but not "The John F. Kennedy." The unpleasantness fortunately would soon pass (with any luck by 10:00 P.M. that same evening), and the society as a whole would stand to gain from the increased levels of effort and the higher prices paid for dinner tickets.

*October 1999*

# *Ars Longa, Vita Brevis*

20 September 1997
Little Marsh Farm
Devon, Pennsylvania

Dear Graydon,

I thought we had finished with the subject of you wanting to become a writer when you passed through New York last April en route to your mother's wedding in Venice. You asked for what you called "an uncle's meddling service," and we spent the better part of an afternoon at a bar on East Tenth Street, talking about your chances of commercial or critical success (nil and next to none), about the number of readers that constitutes the American audience for literature (not enough to fill the seats at Yankee Stadium), about the Q-ratings awarded to authors by the celebrity markets (equivalent to those assigned to trick dogs and retired generals), about the consolations of art (enjoyed posthumously). You didn't disagree with the drift of the conversation, and I thought it was understood that you would apply to business school or pursue the chance of an offer from your friend at Microsoft.

Now I'm told that after you graduate from Stanford next spring you mean to work the Alaskan salmon runs for six months and then travel for two years with a Navajo rock band, gathering notes for the great American road novel. Your mother and I had dinner last night in Philadelphia, and she presented me with your August manifesto, the one in which you describe California as a "desert of materialism" and declare your release from the prison of "store-bought, prerecorded dreams." I'm not sure that I can properly describe your mother's mood. Worried and depressed, but at the same time furious—with your stupidity, my complacence, the mediocrity of the restaurant (not up to the standard to which she's become accustomed in Europe), the day of the week, her nail polish, and the rain. Her questions were mostly rhetorical, asked in a tone of voice with which I'm sure you're familiar:

"Doesn't he know what century he's living in, for God's sake? Has he no sense of what things cost? No ambition? No wish to know the important people in the world?"

No matter how often I explained that I'd made more or less the same points when you and I discussed the prospect of your literary career last spring in Greenwich Village, she refused to be comforted.

"Yes," she said, "but you also told him he had talent . . . that his stories showed signs of promise. You're his only uncle, the only male relative he still trusts, the only person he knows who writes books. What did you expect him to think? That your opinion doesn't count? That you were being supportive and polite, like one of those moth-eaten English professors who discover the mark of genius in any student capable of using the word 'ambiguity' twice in the same paragraph?"

I wasn't being polite, Graydon. Both the stories that you published in the Stanford *Chaparral* show a good deal more promise than most of the fiction that appears in *The New Yorker*, but I shouldn't have said so, and I hope that you will forgive my carelessness. You have a talent for literary expression, but when matched against the trend and spirit of the times it's a superfluous talent—like playing the harpsichord or shooting the Plains buffalo. Amuse yourself with literature when you're older than whoever happens to be president of the United States or rich enough to acquire *The Sewanee Review*. In the meantime, learn to buy hotels.

Before coming to the dessert (a chocolate mousse that your mother pronounced "acceptable") I managed to mollify her with the promise to once again impose upon your patience the wisdom of Polonius. She seemed pleased by my saying that the rock band probably would disintegrate before you boarded the bus in Tucson, but she telephoned the next day from Dulles Airport, reminding me to remind you that she no longer has any appreciable money of her own and that she cannot ask Guelpho to sponsor your literary apprenticeship.

Guelpho apparently hasn't forgiven you for the toast that you proposed at his wedding. ("To my mother's fifth husband, Count Guelpho Faranelli, may he pass and be forgotten with the rest.") Guelpho understands that you were drunk at the time, and it has been explained to him that you intended a complex irony (the jewel of flattery concealed in the glove of insult), but he is not well-versed in the forms of American humor. Neither is he a reader of Flaubert's novels or an admirer of Chekhov's plays. A proud aristocrat, Graydon, who nevertheless yearns to hear you praise his collection of Roman portrait busts and his mastery of the Argentine tango. Antonio Banderas once told him that never in his life had he seen so heavy a man so delicately execute the *paseo de la muerte*. The count cherishes the remark.

It's conceivable, of course, that your manifesto was another complex irony meant to frighten your mother (in the way that boys of your age and disposition sometimes threaten to enlist in the marines or marry a rodeo star), and maybe, like Guelpho, I've failed to guess your intention. But in the event that you might mean at least some of what you say, and by way of making good on my promise to your mother, allow me to review the argument.

The existence of a literature presupposes a literate and coherent public that has both the time to read and a need to take seriously the works of the literary imagination. I'm not sure whether the United States ever had such a public; certainly it hasn't had one for the last thirty years. What we have instead is an opening-night crowd, astonished by celebrity and opulent spectacle, tolerating only those authors who present themselves as freaks and wonders and offer the scandal of their lives as proof of their art. Lacking even one critic whose judgment means anything, the management of the nation's literary affairs falls naturally into the hands of accountants and press agents—i.e., life-forms native to "the deserts of materialism."

Walk into the brightly packaged clutter of the nearest bookstore, and what do you see? Mostly what you would see in *The*

*National Enquirer* or on *Entertainment Tonight*—movie-star gossip, secrets of the pyramids and the stock market, guides to better health, confessions of accomplished swindlers and convicted murderers, beauty tips from notorious madams, the latest bulletins updating the E.T.A. for the end of the world.

If you've been reading the papers, you will have noticed that the publishing business lately has fallen upon hard times. This year's sales for adult trade books (the category you intend to make the canvas of your ambition) have dropped by 12 percent; the bookstores keep new books on their shelves for about the same length of time (five days, maybe two weeks) that grocers keep light cream and sun-dried tomatoes, and they return unsold books to their points of origin at the rate of 45 percent. Which is why even the most literate publishers (the ones who remember that F. Scott Fitzgerald died of drink) seldom take chances with commodities that fail to meet the standards of tabloid journalism and why their best-selling authors turn out to be the kind of people apt to require the services of a capable bail bondsman. When signing the contracts and arranging the publicity, nobody raises a glass of sherry to the memory of Maxwell Perkins. The more subtle the author's thought and the more careful his argument, the smaller his chance of notice. Not enough people will understand what he's trying to say. The shoddy work sells as well as, or better than, the good work, and why confuse the computers in charge of sales with anything other than "store-bought, prerecorded dreams"?

Even those authors whom you admire and presumably consider serious cannot escape the burden of mechanical repetition. Who among them can afford to take chances with a $400,000 advance against royalties and the good opinion of the lecture bureaus? Unless they say what they said last time, how can they become reliable products? The transformation of subject into object serves the interest of the market, but it is a bargain that tends to rob writers of their courage.

If you were a young Englishman at large in the streets of Elizabethan London (an impoverished scholar, say, without land, title, or acquaintance in court), you might have tried your luck as a poet or a playwright. It was an age that delighted in the rush of words to which we now affix the seals and stamps of literature. Conceivably you could have made your way into the circle of patronage surrounding Sir Walter Raleigh or Lord Strange. You might also have been imprisoned for sedition or hanged as a spy, but on the way to the scaffold you at least would have known that you had walked, if only briefly, on the world's stage and that the queen's ministers thought well enough of your wit to kill you for the crime of a well-turned phrase.

So, too, in the nineteenth century, whether in Europe or on the East Coast of America, authors of note commanded the attention of princes and the adulation of the mob. Lord Byron's contemporaries trembled at the approach of his verses; Dickens lectured to crowds not unlike those that now attend concerts by Garth Brooks; all of Boston wept in the presence of Emerson's sermons; Victor Hugo could have been elected president of France.

During the first half of the twentieth century the figure of the literary hero retained an aura of power and authority—think of James Joyce, of Thomas Mann, or Ernest Hemingway as *The Old*

*Man and the Sea*—but the role has been rendered irrelevant by television and the hydrogen bomb, reduced to farce by Norman Mailer's traipsing around the department-store book-signing circuit dressed up in the persona of King Lear.

The literary crowd likes to mourn the death of the written word and regret the disappearance of "public intellectuals" who supposedly once led the readers of American newspapers, like a flock of confused sheep, into the pastures of enlightenment. The familiar dirge can be best understood as advertising promotion. It isn't that the modern world has abandoned the written word but rather that certain kinds of literary usage or construction have lost their currency and force. The surge of human intellect always flows into the sea of public event, but in the late twentieth century the rivers of expression drain the uplands of the sciences and the watersheds of the film and computer technologies. People ask the questions they deem important (What is man? Why do I have to die?) not of poets or novelists but of chemists and cosmetic surgeons.

HBO and prime-time television offer the rewards of both fame and fortune that long ago and once upon a time attracted the Cambridge wits to the Elizabethan stage, and were Shakespeare now alive on St. Crispin's Day you could expect to find him arranging the play of light and shadow in a Hollywood movie studio. A Wall Street investment bank composes a seventeen-page prospectus laying out the plot for the merger of two pharmaceutical companies, and its author's fee comes up to an amount (maybe $4 million, possibly as much as $10 million) that dwarfs the earnings of all the books enrolled on any season's bestseller list. The sums that large corporations routinely allot every year to upgrading their communications systems exceed, by a multiple of four, the annual subsidies grudgingly donated to the National Endowments for the Humanities and the Arts. I've known lawyers to compose trust agreements with as many tiers of hidden meaning as can be found in Herman Melville's chapter on the whiteness of Moby Dick.

Last winter when the Clinton Administration identified the 831 guests who had stayed overnight in the White House, did you see the names of any writers on the list? Steven Spielberg dropped by, and so did Barbra Streisand and Tom Hanks, but where was Thomas Pynchon? The President has seen *High Noon* no fewer than twenty times. How many times do you think he's read *The Crying of Lot 49?* I don't wish to bore you with the obvious, Graydon, but when have you seen a writer on a golf course with Michael Jordan, on the screen with Ted Koppel, on the cover of *Vanity Fair?*

Which is, I think, your mother's principal objection to your thesis of a literary career. Where's the glamour in it? The hope of adventure? The chance of an appearance in the gossip columns? Within the ghetto of the literary life, the money is small, the accommodations poor, the circle of acquaintance necessarily limited (like that of a motorcycle or kennel club), the conversation paranoid, the people almost never pretty.

Your mother tends to exaggerate the importance of appearances (one of her traits of character that both of us must hope Count Faranelli finds endearing), and when she speaks of writers as persons uniformly "sallow, bitter, self-preoccupied, envious, furtive, and drab," she overstates her point. It's not true that all writers lurk in corners gnawing on old cocktail cheese. I've known writers who dine on pheasant. Some of them stand in the center of the room. A few of them write remarkable books.

But neither is your mother entirely wrong. Why squander your talent and intelligence on a career that leads, even under the best of circumstances, nowhere but into the footnoted gloom of one of the country's neo-Gothic universities? Fast-forward the calendar to the year 2027 and grant yourself the unlikely favor of literary success—the author of four novels critically acclaimed on three continents (none of which sold more than 15,000 copies in hardcover and 40,000 in paper), celebrated by *Newsweek* as "the poet of despair" and by *Time* as "the conscience of the age," writer in residence at Duke, occasional but esteemed contributor to *The New York Review of Books*, sought after by the sponsors of summer creative-writing programs, the lion of Bread Loaf—groomed by librarians, cosseted by graduate students, fed from the dish of foundation grants.

All well and good and devoutly to be wished, but to what purpose? Books have so little to do with the business of America that the writers who aspire to the status of literary trademarks reserve their most vivid narratives to the story of the self. But if it is the life and not the book that becomes the work of art, why go to the intermediate trouble of constructing sentences instead of leveraged-buyout deals?

Become a partner at Salomon Brothers, write episodes of *Seinfeld* or jokes for David Letterman, speculate on the Shanghai Stock

Exchange, sell music videos to the Russians, curry favor with George Soros, but keep thy foot out of English departments and flee the company of young women familiar with the names of Joseph Conrad and Marcel Proust.

Work the Alaska salmon run or wander with the Navajo, but do so because you wish to travel, not because you plan to write a book. Make the mistake of thinking that you can decide to become a writer and you've already lost the bet. Writers happen by accident, not by design. They have as little choice in the matter as lemmings toppling over cliffs. If and when the spirit moves you (and you find yourself being drawn irretrievably to the sea), it won't occur to you to ask or heed anybody's advice, least of all that of your fond and word-ridden uncle,

Dyer

*October 1997*